A MARINE'S STORY

A MARINE'S STORY

"OKAY, BUDDY, LET'S GO! HOORAH!"
A Marine Sniper Survives Vietnam

Told by Michael T. Smith
Written by Phil Lenser

ISBN: 9798843423414

TABLE OF CONTENTS

PREFACE

One Sunday after church, our congregation moved from the sanctuary into the social hall for a time of fellowship and food. Churches love to have their members getting closer to each other and learning together how to live out their common faith. One of the chefs this Sunday wore a black apron with a Marine Corps emblem nearly filling the bib. Even though my wife and I have attended this church for over ten years and our congregation is smallish at perhaps a couple hundred people, I had never been introduced to this gentleman. He looked to be close to my age. Okay, maybe he was a few years older.

Being a Marine myself, I started with "Semper Fi." It's short for semper fidelis, the Latin phrase meaning "always faithful." Always faithful to myself, my country, and my corps. It's the Marine Corps motto, this shortened version being a common Marine-to-Marine greeting. I have had a few veterans of other services also use the greeting, and even some of my civilian friends use it as well, knowing I smile when they do.

The words "Semper Fi" convey a commitment that is easy to repeat; it's much tougher to live out.

My years were 1972 to 1977. I always wanted to fly. Dad had been a B-17 bombardier in WWII. While still in high school, I saw an article in a news magazine about Reserve Officer Training Corps (ROTC) scholarships. It said there were thousands of them. I applied and was awarded a United States Air Force scholarship. Four years, Oregon State. Flight training during summers as you progress. It was one of the best scholarships of my rural northern California high school in 1969. That summer, a "friend" wrecked his uncle's '68 Mustang evading an unmarked cop car with me in the passenger seat sitting just behind the impact point with the telephone pole. My two broken legs meant I would not be healed by the start of the next semester. The scholarship was awarded to the alternate.

A few years later, the brother of a girl I had met after I landed at the local JC instead of Oregon State told me the Marine Corps was offering a two-year aviation commissioning program. This program offered flight-qualified applicants with two years of undergraduate credits a chance at Officer Candidate School (OCS), and then on to naval flight training in Pensacola to learn to fly Marine jets. That's where all of us as we applied thought we were heading—to fly jets. I thought, *Wow, officer training, flight school, and jets all with only two years of college.* And as a bonus, signing up would make me ineligible for the draft.

Then, I realized the first step was Marine Corps Officer Candidate School. This brother of the girl I met at school; he had done it. But he was a stud. And he wasn't going aviation; he became a grunt platoon commander. He told me if I wanted to do it, he believed I could. And he said, "You better start running. When you get to OCS, if you can keep up with the runs, you'll be way ahead."

We had the draft lottery in those years. A random chance to have your number drawn. The year of my eligibility, we all stayed up late waiting to see the draw and hear when our date of birth was picked. Your lottery number was where your birthday was selected in the sequence of draws. Draft boards started calling people up starting with one and progressed through something like 150 to maybe 180. If your number came up after 180, the further out, the safer from the draft you would be.

My birthday was drawn at fifty-one.

Sure enough, it turned out that by enlisting in the Marine Corps aviation program, I avoided being drafted. My notice to report arrived about three weeks after I signed with my OSO (Officer Selection Officer). Had I been drafted, it's likely I would have been in the army. Who knows? Maybe I'd have gone directly to Vietnam. Maybe it would have been me carrying an M16 in the jungle. Probably I would have been there in 1971 or '72. Too many Americans my age died in Vietnam. As it was, with OCS and then over a year of flight school, I would not be eligible for overseas deployment until 1975, the year of our withdrawal from Saigon. My squadron was there when I got to WESTPAC. The guys I came to know and fly with had flown out all those they could as people tried to escape from our embassy.

I was one of the forty-two that completed OCS out of the fifty-one in our first formation. I found the Marine Corps to be appropriately serious about the training and character of their officers.

At flight school, I was selected for helicopters. Yes, that meant some of my peers were better pilots than I had become. Having never flown anything except in my dreams; having never actually sat in a cockpit and having never touched any flight controls with my own hands or feet before the service, I was pleased to have a set of wings. Have you ever seen the panel of instruments in a military aircraft? Me either.

Through a fluke, the group commander as we were reporting for assignment to my first transport helicopter squadron offered me and another new-to-the-fleet rookie pilot the option of switching assignments from transports to Cobras or Hueys. I elected Cobras and spent my next three years flying the Spitfire of the helicopter world. The snake is a narrow, two-pilot, tandem-seated helicopter gunship with a 20 mm Gatling gun ready to spew two thousand rounds per minute from the full-flex nose turret out front. The airframe is equipped with four stubbed-wing ordnance mounting stations, each capable of carrying a variety of configurations but most commonly armed with pods of nineteen rockets each. That's seventy-six rockets. This baby is the fastest, most maneuverable helicopter in the fleet and is entirely about close-in air support for our Marines. An airborne fire breather. Such a rush.

In my years, I'd be in the air flying most days or studying up on the next evolution in our training or preparing for the next deployment. We worked at being ready. I missed the war. No one ever shot at me. I was never asked to shoot at anyone. Thank God. Lucky timing.

That day at church, Mike Smith introduced himself and told me he had served in Vietnam in 1968–1970. He told me he was a scout/sniper. I thought, *Wow, that's a brutal job.* He told me he had gone to sniper school, and one of his instructors was Carlos Hathcock. I knew Carlos's name. He is known to Marines. He is famous. Carlos held the sniper record in Vietnam. He had killed hundreds. He was known for distance, accuracy, and of course, stealth. People talked about him and what he had done.

By the way, in the scout/sniper community, they don't refer to kills as kills. Too crass. They talk "assignments."

Then Mike told me a short version of his story in just a few minutes.

I knew he had to have a story because he was standing in front of me. Marine snipers serving in times of war are kept busy doing their duty and trying to survive. Here he was, standing there a survivor. I heard an incredible story. I wanted to know more. How did he learn to shoot so well? What was Carlos like? How do you live with having killed people? Aren't you terrified? I couldn't believe what he told me. It seemed impossible, yet as I asked him to tell me more of the details and as more of his story was revealed, the more I felt others needed to hear what had happened and what he did. Mike is a hero. Like many other heroes, he doesn't think so.

Because we are both Marines, and maybe because I instantly raved about how amazing and heroic he is, Mike felt open and comfortable talking about his combat stuff with me even when I challenged some of what he said or some of what they did. Mike told me more details than he had ever told anyone.

And as we talked, strange things came out. Over forty years after, as he was going about his everyday normal just before retirement life, suddenly he discovers he had been awarded a very significant combat citation for what had happened. The Bronze Star. It had never been claimed. A guy on a base helped him file a request for it. It arrived by mail. Having heard Mike telling the story of what had happened, I was pleased for him, too.

How had all of this affected Mike? Did he carry scars from what he experienced? Yes, he definitely has external physical scars and he carries some internal emotional ones as well. Can providing him the opportunity to tell the story so it can be written down be therapeutic? Can having the story told help other veterans? Can those that have never served but wonder what it is like to be in a war feel some of the emotion, some of the adrenalin, some of the deep inner effects and scars these men endure? We agreed, we'd give it a try.

I wondered what I would have done in his shoes. Could I have come close to his effort, his sacrifice, his coping with what had occurred? As you read, maybe you will wonder too.

Now that I've heard it all from Mike and written it out for him and for you, I'm pleased you are about to jump in. Read on. Enjoy.
Semper Fi!

Note to readers: The story ahead is laid out in much the same chronological sequence I heard Mike telling it to me. Travel with him now as he heads out on his final mission and then into what happened immediately afterward. Then we fast forward to one of the final conversations he and I had, where we focused on what had happened, what Mike had done, and who should have responsibility or guilt for what happened. As you may have noted in the table of contents, next we offer for those that want to know more about how this all came to be: Mike's growing-up years, his being drafted, and his training as a Marine. Finally, the conversations we had bringing out more details complete his story.

FOREWORD

Mike Smith was just out of high school at nineteen, busily working on getting his young adult life going, when the notice to report arrived. While he was growing up, his dad had taught him how to hunt, and in the process, he learned to be an amazing shot. He was much better with a rifle, especially at long distances, than most trained marksmen. The Marines saw Mike's rifle skills. They gave him advanced training in a school that included Carlos Hathcock, the best Marine sniper of that day, as one of his instructors. Mike was soon on the ground in the jungle serving in Vietnam in the midst of the war. In one of his years, 11,780 Americans died. If you graduated high school in those years, several guys whose pictures are in your yearbook were killed. It's too big a number to relate to when you consider the pain of even one death. But on average, over thirty guys were killed each day, every day. Dead. Funerals happened all over the country. Most of those guys were nineteen or twenty when they died. Most of Mike's tour was during that terrible year, his final mission in January 1970.

The story and bonus conversations let us sit in on two Marines talking through what happened to Mike, what his life in Vietnam was like, and some of the ways he has dealt with what happened to him in his war.

Teaser of the story ahead:

Relax. Focus. Follow the truck's path. Watch for the target. Slow your breath.

The instant collapse followed by the crack of this single round interrupting the morning quiet was such a shock, so abrupt, so isolated the guards feel powerless.

Keep crawling. Elbows raw. Right knee bruised and bloody.

These amazing pilots that drove this angel helicopter out here to come searching for him and his green smoke don't even realize they're making his lifesaving rescue ride to safety in these fragments of moments a tiny measure of hell.

"Mike, you did all you could have."

Final Mission Part One

January 9, 1970

About midnight, Marine Scout/Sniper, Corporal Michael T. Smith, and his spotter, Private First Class Jonathan Rogers, walk silently from the ready area out to the waiting Huey. Their faces are painted with black and green grease. Their eyes peer out from under their floppy, wide-brimmed boonie hats. Their utilities bear no rank, no identification, no insignia of any kind. They wear no dog tags. They carry M1A1 Super Match tricked-out sniper-modified M14s. Their battle vests contain four magazines, each loaded with twenty rounds of 7.62 ammo. A razor-sharp K bar knife hangs at easy reach, sheathed at their shoulders. The knife's handle is the size of an extra-large screwdriver, the inch-wide blade extending nearly six wicked inches long.

A holster with a .45 pistol, two backup magazines each of seven rounds, and a canteen are riding on their cartridge belts. Smith's rifle is equipped with a nine-times-magnification scope. Rogers carries a twenty-times sighting glass. Pockets in their vests contain personal medical items: sulfa powder, field bandages, and syrettes of morphine. Camouflaging Ghillie suits to wear in the hide are ready in a bag slung under an arm.

The rpms of the turbine engines whine, the rotors come whipping up as they accelerate to full speed. The pilot grasps and smoothly pulls the collective (power and pitch) up with his left hand, pausing instinctively at just the edge of lift, creating a moment of poised, alert balance in the chopper. The Huey's airframe lifts up, still sitting firmly on its skids, and gets light and tall, ready to rise on command into a stable, balanced hover. It's all perked up, tensed and coiled like a runner who has heard the call of "ready, set" and is eagerly waiting for the starting gun to leap forward.

The skipper pulls more collective with his left hand while finding the magic balance point over their spot with the cyclic in his right. His control inputs neutralize the twists and thrusts on the airframe with the light touch of his boots teetering on the rudder pedals. His fanny is belted in the seat. Both hands and both feet are moving the flight controls in those smooth, subtle, and precise motions. These inputs control the aircraft's chaos, taming the counter forces of the torque, the rotors, and the random breeze or sudden gusts of wind. The Huey lifts vertically straight up into a hover with the airframe taking on its slightly nose-down airborne attitude. They are flying. These pilots are seasoned. There is no rookie tail wiggle, no novice hover bounce. She comes straight up; they feel her into the air. They are flying with totally controlled stability an aircraft of inherent instability. The chopper crew pauses for a moment to visually check systems, instrument panel caution lights, and for the right readings in the needles of the gauges. The skipper gets clearance for launch from the control tower, returns the sendoff salute from the flight line crew chief, then rolls nose down as they begin to accelerate, sliding forward and up. They climb higher, flying faster and faster as they soar out into the night and toward their mission.

This trip is all business. Marine Corps business.

This scout/sniper team has an assignment. An assignment only fully known to them.

Cpl. Smith and Pfc. Rogers had listened intently in the briefing. This assignment is a senior North Vietnamese Army (NVA) officer, a colonel. He has a ruthless reputation and commands hundreds of enemy troops. They have been briefed on where he is headed, and they are going to be there, waiting, ahead of him. They have it all planed. One shot, one kill.

There are no external lights on the chopper; the only illumination coming from the slightly less than quarter moon peeking through the clouds of the night sky. Inside the cockpit and in the crew cabin where Smith and Rogers are now riding, there is only the soft red glow of the instrument panel lights. It's a cool, dark night with a light, misty rain falling from scattered clouds hanging over the valley.

Even when seen at night, the brilliance and beauty of Vietnam with its glowing, lustrous lime-green accent shades gleaming through on the deeper and darker background greens of the jungle when seen in this type of wonderous panoramic motion picture viewed from an airborne Huey while it gallops through the sky, has a feel many GIs take home from their tour. That and the beat, beat, beat of the rotor, the roar of the turbines, and the bounce of the ride as they slip over the rice paddies, roads, and trails heading toward the mountains to the west. For the next few moments of this flight on its way out to their drop-off, they are safe but still keenly alert and tense. Mike is already working out in his mind step by step how he will lead them through the jungle and toward their objective. The aerial photos he has memorized had shown where the mansion sat in the valley they will be hiking into.

The chopper flies solo, a bit north and west about half an hour.

The Huey slows and slips down toward a flat, open field a few hundred yards from the jungle and Laos. On the descent, the aircraft makes a precautionary clearing turn going around in a 360-degree circle above the landing zone (LZ), trying in the process to draw out any enemy who may be nearby. When there is no incoming fire, the pilots work their instruments and the moonlight as they slip the Huey lower toward the wide-open field of the rice patty, thereby allowing themselves lots of room to get stable in a hover before they taxi forward to the drop-off point. Even good sticks can pucker up a bit at an attempt to hover with just the sweet light of the moon. In these slivers of moonlight, it's tough to see the horizon and the good earth below. Pilots need to make visual contact as they descend and often don't achieve it until less than thirty feet off the deck. Every night, these pilots insert without lights. They are good and are getting better, helped by confidence born out of their youth, bravado, and training. Of course, they also have been trained to be head's up during the weather briefing for the phase and positioning of the moon. If possible, flight operations will time their inserts to maximize its glow to their benefit and advantage.

On the descent, Mike and Jonathan load magazines, chamber a round, and set safeties. Smith and Rogers are locked and loaded. They both take a few sips from the duty canteen the crew chief filled for their use, thereby saving the water they carry in the canteens on their hips for the mission ahead. They scooch down, sitting on the floor, and dangle their legs out the left doorway, the fields below sliding by as the airstream blasts their faces, flapping at their uniforms. They rest their boots on the skids and hold steady, waiting and ready to jump out on the crew chief's signal.

A bit over a week earlier, Smith had volunteered for this assignment and had argued that he should conduct this mission alone. On his own. Cpl. Smith believed it would be safer for him—safer for the mission—if he operated alone. His mentor and role model, Carlos Hathcock, had conducted many similar assignments totally alone. But too many other scout/snipers operating alone had failed to return. Battalion commanders had changed standard operating procedure (SOP), hoping to lose fewer resources. Now, scout/snipers could only operate alone in the rare low-risk assignment. This one was not one of those.

His OIC (officer in charge) listened to Mike's request to operate solo, shook his head, and ordered that a spotter go along. Marines only argue with the OIC once and never when under fire.

Mike had worked with several spotters before. When told he would not be alone, that he would have a spotter for this assignment, he had begun to ask for his buddy, Jonathan. Jonathan was already standing by, having been placed on alert. Now he was tapped and called into the briefing.

Mike would never say so directly to him, but he liked the kid. He liked the way Jonathan handled himself in the jungle. He was quiet. He did what he was told. He knew how to hide, how to move, and how to say what needed to be said without a word leaving his lips. He helped Mike with the mechanics of targeting their assignment, estimating distances, and having several alternative targeting scenarios thought out and ready. You never know in advance which way your assignment will turn.

For his part, Jonathan had watched Mike work. He was impressed. He had already seen amazing shooting. It seemed that each time Mike took aim, he got better. Jonathan's eyes were filled with awe and respect. He liked being with Mike. They were becoming a great team.

Mike and Jonathan heard enough at the briefing to conclude that the individual assigned as the target on this assignment is indeed a righteous target. In addition to being a senior officer commanding enemy troops, this guy is the instigator behind the evil of using village kids to blow up GIs.

Somehow, the NVA were commandeering and training six-to-eight-year-old kids. The kids were sent onto US bases.

Little kids are welcomed by Americans, often with a quick smile and the offer of a Hershey bar.

The kids were taught to pull the pin and release the spoon as the GI got close.

When a hand grenade erupts, it sprays hundreds of ragged metal shrapnel fragments everywhere with its explosion. This mass of randomly flying blades violently rip, tear, and penetrate any nearby body, frequently causing massive trauma and multiple horrific, bloody wounds. Everything within ten to fifteen feet is hit. Blown apart. Sometimes it's a fast death. Sometimes slow. Nearly a third of US casualties in Vietnam are from blasts. Grenades, mortars, bombs, that kind of stuff.

Many US and South Vietnamese troops die a gruesome, painful grenade death. Many innocent kids discover too late what happens when they do what they had been taught, going down screaming in agony and terror too.

The survivors in the local villages, the families and the friends, are left mourning in unquenchable, perpetual grief over lost sons and daughters. Death of a dearly loved young one is a never-ending ache everywhere on the planet.

Many villagers hate the NVA. Most of them only do the NVA's bidding out of fear and intimidation. That's one reason you can never trust a local. They are often facing beatings, torture, or in way too many cases death. Those that were seen talking with Americans frequently did not survive the night.

When Mike and Jonathan heard the story in the briefing of the kids, they were immediately sickened, disgusted, and pissed. They recognized who this was. They've heard the reports of kids blowing themselves up. They know of several occasions on nearby bases and camps when some of the local little kids had blown themselves and whoever was nearby to pieces. They've heard and read these reports for months now. Good guys had gone down. Everyone despised this guy. Maybe getting the colonel would slow or stop the grenade/kid evil. They all want someone to get him.

Mike and Jonathan both were agreed and quick to say, "Yes, we'll go."

Every briefing is offering a voluntary assignment. A Marine scout/sniper team can refuse or bail on any mission for any reason, anytime. No questions asked. Scout/snipers only go when they have confidence that the assignment can be completed and that they will survive. They go planning that they'll come home from it. They count on it. They carefully prepare for it. Sometimes, things happen. Things they didn't foresee.

The crew chief gives a quick tap on Mike's shoulder as the chopper slows to a hovering pause just a few feet or five off the deck. Smith and Rogers stand, step out, free falling forward with all their gear strapped and stowed, their weapons held protectively at an angle across their chests, and, of course, with their knees bent for the coming impact, collapse, and roll. They hit the wet field and crumple like they have been trained, flopping onto the grass and mud. The Huey immediately lifts from its low hover and turns tightly as it climbs, going away back over their heads.

The blast of the rotor wash subsides, the whine of the turbines recedes, and the woop-woop-woop of the blades fades as the chopper moves further away, becoming smaller, eventually going out of sight. The night gets quiet, still, dark, damp, and cool. Now, it's just these two. They lay in the mud staying very still for the next few moments. They breathe softly, silently listening. Their primal senses are on alert. Intensely.

They hear nothing. It's quiet. They're alone. They hope totally alone.

Smith and Rogers know where they are going. They have been near here before. Prior missions have been several clicks north up the valley they are about to start moving toward. A click is a kilometer. Military maps are scaled in kilometers, thus Marines measure distance in clicks. It's through the jungle on the west end of the rice fields. It's across the border.

Smith jumps up and leads into the dark, across the field and into the thick jungle. No words. Hand signals only. There's enough light to stay together without needing to use the nylon line they brought to maintain contact if there wasn't.

Their inner voices remind them: *stay off paths, take your time, and settle down.* Each step is made like a stalking cat, their toes tilting forward like a paw as they creep slowly through the brush and grass. *No hurry.* All senses are on high alert. Look, listen, hear, touch, feel, and taste the jungle and the night. January in Laos is over eighty degrees mostly, rain just here or about to come. Damp, humid, and smelling of that recent rain, the jungle's freshness and quiet is calming, giving them a sense of ease while they also feel keenly on edge. They move as one, staying almost in the same footprints as Jonathan sticks to and shadows Mike.

In a bit over three hours, they cover the four clicks to the edge of the clearing near the target location. Four clicks are just over two and a half miles. Mike is good at slowly maneuvering them in the optimal direction to their preplanned position using his well-tuned mountaineering skills. Compass in hand, he is plotting his moves so that they will emerge in the valley on the other side knowing which way to turn to move even closer to the target. The maps and photos he diligently studied are implanted at the ready in his mind.

While it's still night with just the sliver of moon and the flickering stars giving light, somewhere between 0330 and 0400 (3:30 a.m. and 4:00 a.m. respectively), they stop at the jungle's edge to wet their whistles and take a whiz. They peel off and stuff their boonie hats in as they pull out and don the Ghillie suits. They have routines. This time they will be lying in an open field of tropical jungle grass. The stuff is thick and tall, in some places over three feet tall. They both use their knives to cut some of the green growing around them. They add these blades of grass and leaves to their suits, enhancing their ability to camouflage and blend in. When each is happy with the other's look, they squat down and then belly crawl slowly in silence onto a knoll. They had identified the knoll on their maps and know instinctively from prior assignments that this location would be ideal, given its unrestricted view and very slight elevation above the open fields fronting the building on the other side. From here the view of the potential target area will be wide open. The rising sun will come up behind them, giving their target illumination and offering their position additional cover. They flatten out and low crawl on their forearms/elbows and thighs/knees until they are in position. They want to be close enough for the one shot and far enough to never be detected or seen.

They blend in becoming a part of the landscape, listening, observing, and waiting. Daybreak is a couple hours away. They are lying in the dirt and grass of the dew-covered fields just beyond the edge of the jungle. They settle in and become even more undetectable. Invisible.

At this distance, Mike's one shot will be taken from a prone, stable frame. He extends his weapon's bipod, settling in to wait. As usual, they are early and ready. Mike rolls onto his back, turning face up for a time, allowing his eyes to rest for these few moments before daybreak. He slows his breathing, closes his eyes, and tries to relax. Jonathan keeps watch.

When the sun begins to crest behind them, Mike rolls back into the rifle, shouldering it gently as he scans through his scope. Jonathan peers through the field glass. So far, only outlines and silhouettes are visible.

Daybreak is coming. Gradually, terrain begins to emerge.

The mansion appears out of the morning mist and shadows.

It's a beautiful whitewashed two-story colonial home. It was probably built as a residence for some well-to-do French settler and family. Over the years since, it has served as a haven for the wealthy and the well connected. Now, it has been converted to a resort. It's the only structure in this valley, a long way off by itself. No village or other nearby homes share its grounds, just the work areas and storage sheds of the caretakers and staff. It's surrounded by open fields of rice, offering its guests a gorgeous, picturesque vista sitting just this side of the jungle with mountains rising behind in glorious tropical green.

This mansion has also become an occasional sanctuary for North Vietnamese officers who have earned a few days of liberty away from war.

They come here to take a breather and relax. For the next few days, they will enjoy fine food and liberal spirits. Their conversations will include war stories, exaggerations, lies, and laughs with their buddies. For many, the primary draw and reward of the mansion is the presence and company of ladies of pleasure. While here, they will have ready access to willing companionship. On request, as much as they like. The mansion has a dozen "attractive" ladies in attendance ready to please.

The intelligence briefing had said the target of this assignment would likely be arriving today. Sometime. Maybe. More than maybe, very likely. His name was on a list having earned a reservation, but some unknown operational need in his unit might at the last minute get in the way and push his liberty out a week or two. So very likely today.

Smith and Rogers spot movement. Enemy sentries are walking posts. Some have dogs.

At this distance, it's hard to see much detail. Even with the magnification of Mike's scope or Jonathan's sighting glass, the views of the sentries are distant and fuzzy, like looking at a figure out nearly to the opposite end of a football field. When it comes time to engage, Mike's aim is going to need to be steady. Very steady.

Most of the sentries have their rifles slung over a shoulder, their heads looking down or bobbing from side to side as they walk out their all-night watch. In total, Mike and Jonathan spot six NVA troopers walking their posts, looking tired, hungry, and bored. Several look beat and loaded; turns out most of them are.

In the mix, there are three dogs. Rottweilers on leash with some of the sentries. They're smart, quick, and vicious.

Smith and Rogers stay far enough, still enough, and quiet enough that the dogs don't sense their presence.

In preparation for this mission and the Rottweilers, both Smith and Rogers have consumed what the locals consume for the last ten days. They want their sweat to smell the way locals do. Their diet became whole fried insects, mostly the jumbo grasshoppers that are common to Asian jungles. Add some narrow strips of grilled local fish that have a crazy, make-your-face-frown slimy bitterness on the tongue. Just a totally uber-salty taste. Add some boiled jungle tuber roots and a handful of steamed brown field rice. Then blend it all with a repugnant black sauce mixture of pungent ginger, local herbs, and tropical spices. Mike and Jonathan had held the bowl to their mouths, trying to ignore the sour odor, and shoveled with chopsticks day by day. They want to eat enough for long enough so that their sweat gives off local body smells. They want their fragrance to blend in. Stink like they stink. Some of the flavors are repulsive, almost gagging, especially the extra heavy doses of ginger. At first, throwing a fried overgrown grasshopper (or even part of it) into your mouth is gross. A bit gagging. *Yuck.* The sound of the crunch of its body resonating in your cheek takes getting used to. Its feel on your tongue, the tiny bug bits in your teeth, it's some crazy combination of new flavors and textures. Something decidedly not fun but they were told necessary. Swallowing the tissue is not a big deal after you have experienced a few gags trying. Still, Carlos had taught Cpl. Smith that having American odors could give him away. Ten days on the local diet was one of his mantras for survival. Carlos—in his thinking, in his actions, and in his teachings—was all about survival. And he says, "Remember, the locals eat the same thing every day, and they like it." Mike and Jonathan never got to like it.

Mike and Jonathan feel the tension of the constant flow of adrenaline, every sense on edge. Hairs stand on end, even as they try to relax and wait.

They go about their routines, picking out reference points, estimating distances, looking for signs of wind, and determining what adjustments Mike needs in the aiming point. All by hand signal. No whispering, no sound.

Mike estimates seven hundred yards. Jonathan signals with his fingers that he sees it as 680. It's interesting that they are quibbling over twenty yards. This is a ridiculous distance for any shooter who has ever actually tried shouldering a high-powered rifle and shooting at a range of more than 200 yards. Even with a scope, if you have ever tried, this distance sounds just nuts. This assignment will be out nearly seven football fields, or about four tenths of a mile. Using the odometer in the family car to get a sense of this range and watching that little dial turn as you go, you will pass by more than two long blocks traveling this distance in most towns.

It's as far as two decent par three golf holes laid out end on end. So if you are standing on the tee box of the first, you would be looking at the second flag out beyond your current hole through your scope. The flag on the pin at the hole way out there is about the size of your target. Only the target will be a bit smaller than the flag and not as tall.

It's a speck in your scope. This incredible distance is much further than what some scout/snipers would work. Mike likes the extra portion of safety the added distance provides, especially given the size of the detail of NVA sentries and their dogs on alert. It's true, the distance makes their attack more challenging, but it also increases the safety margin for their escape. Mike had learned to always plan his escape before taking any shot. At 300 yards, for him, it would be a cinch. At 500 yards, still a natural. At this 680 yards, Mike has confidence.

Marine scout/snipers train for one shot, one kill. Smith has confidence that, yes, even at this healthy distance, his skills, his precision, his one shot will do the job.

Jonathan has seen Mike's remarkable marksmanship on display. He has seen Mike on the range at one thousand yards. His group of ten rounds all left holes within a hand's width of each other. Nice tight pattern.

Two days ago, he watched Mike as they took their regular practice rounds at the edge of their camp. Mike had Jonathan start by taking a spotting shot at a random tree a healthy distance out to set a target for him to work. Then as the spotter watched intently, Mike eased down until prone, settling smoothly into his aiming posture and grip. He calmly sighted in, took a half breath, exhaled half out, gently squeezed his trigger, and hit the same tree, same limb within inches. Bingo. Amazing. He was on. One with the rifle.

Jonathan had been beside Mike on their three prior assignments. As Mike's spotter, one responsibility is to observe the point of impact of each round Mike fires. Part of Jonathan's duty is to suggest adjustments and corrections. Shooters see the immediate results of their shots microseconds after the round is fired while spotters see the entire flight of each round and the actual impact. The recoil of the weapon spares the shooter of some of that view. Jonathan's role is to watch and if needed to adjust. That is his primary duty. Of course, he needs to keep in mind that at these distances, even tiny tweaks can easily translate to several inches or more. As he watched, Jonathan had noticed as well, Mike seemed to be even better on real, living, moving enemy targets. He had a hunter's training and instincts. And now all of that has been polished with his time in combat to a level nearing perfection.

Jonathan had been beside Mike as they hunted those three prior soldiers. He watched each ones head slammed and then their bodies drop. More than drop, they had collapsed, toppling, and crumpling over instantly dead. He saw it all through his twenty-times sighting glass.

He saw all too clearly where each round Mike had fired impacted each one of the three. Mike was hitting where he aimed, where he intended. Not just head shots. Eye-level head shots. All three of those NVA soldiers, those men, were now eliminated. Gone. Good job.

Yes, Jonathan had seen each of those kills. He can't stop seeing them. After each of those assignments he had withdrawn from their ambush position by hiking through the jungle following Mike's every step. Each time, Mike and Jonathan had grunted silently the way Marines do and smiled at their success. Each time, they both had felt accomplishment, satisfaction, and immense relief at having the assignment completed. Hoorah! Each time, it took several hours afterwards for them to settle down. After each assignment, when the night came, they laid alone sleepless, listening in the dark. Their eyes wanted to stay open, staring into the nothing, as they waited for calm, longing for sleep.

With each successfully completed assignment, both Marines' eyes, posture, and bearing morphs. They sought to successfully complete each assignment, knowing that meant seeing their targets violent death. They begin to carry the physical burden and mark of what they are doing and what they have seen. They have that look about their eyes that tells others they have experienced combat. They have seen men killed. Killed by them.

Jonathan had heard talk about Smith before being assigned. Mike's long-distance marksmanship skills are good enough that people talked. Now, he has seen those three NVA leaders drop and is with Mike as his second set of eyes for this fourth time. He is Mike's spotter and his witness. Jonathan is making Mike better. As a team, they are clicking.

Cpl. Smith has been at it for over a year and a half now. He is professional. He's 100 percent. At the end of his first tour, when he was asked, he proudly and without hesitation volunteered to re-up and stay at it. He knew what he was about. He was saving others.

And honestly, Jonathan likes that Mike listens to him. Well, mostly seems to listen. Okay, sometimes listens.

Jonathan has seen that his observations and suggestions have had influence on Mike. Adjustments have been made. They are a team.

Jonathan feels a whole lot safer with Mike and very grateful to be assigned to shadow him. It's a relief to be away from the grunts. This risk is less than that greater risk. Yes, he will be part of a team killing the enemy, but he's not a grunt. Grunts go out on patrol looking for a gunfight, and they are good at finding gunfights. But they don't ever stop after one and come back to camp. In fact, they rarely come back to camp. The only ones helo'd out are WIA or KIA. Day after day hunting, killing, and hoping to survive. People with guns are chasing you and often shooting at you from too close. Grunts stay out, resupply what they need from the air, and keep going. Surviving as a grunt today means you get more of the same tomorrow. This spotter job was better. Much better. Jonathan knew he was doing better at staying beside Mike, out of his way, and quiet.

Morning is breaking. No target yet in sight.

Jonathan, off on Mike's right, lowers his glass, points, and mouths without sound, "Dust."

A truck is coming.

Mike thinks to himself: *Relax. Focus. Follow the truck's path. Watch for the target. Slow your breath.*

The North Vietnamese colonel who ordered his subordinates to con little kids from the local villages into carrying grenades bounds out of the truck as it comes to a stop.

With jerking body motions as he flings his arms and legs a bit like a banty rooster, the colonel strides toward the entrance to the mansion while barking reprimands to the nearest sentries. Back during the briefing, the agent for this mission had said, "This guy has an angry attitude. He's naturally spring loaded to the pissed off." Sure enough, that's just what Mike and Jonathan are seeing.

Smith watches the officer's movement, focusing his crosshairs and flowing his aiming point moving ever so subtly in sync along with the bounces, keeping "the spot" locked at the ideal gap above mid forehead.

It's 680 yards by Jonathan; Mike's sights are hard set for four hundred. Carlos had taught hard setting sights at the most common mission distance; thus, he was hard set at four hundred yards. Scopes come equipped with adjustment knobs. Turning either the vertical or horizontal crosshair knob moves the aiming point equivalent to the shooter's calculations for wind (vertical) or distance (horizontal). The knobs have an audible click and the feeling of an indentation to the finger and thumb as they are turned. The click is not loud, but there is a click.

Carlos hated any sound. He hated the sound of the click. Sound betrays the scout/sniper. Sound invites detection, capture, and death. Besides, turning the knob takes too much time and is nearly impossible to do when the sniper is in a hide, especially when lying down. Carlos trained, "Hard set them and adjust your aim. That's all. Do not fiddle with those dumb knobs."

At this greater than four-hundred-yard distance, Mike knows from his study of ballistics that the flying 7.62mm round will drop maybe a couple or three inches. To adjust for the drop, Mike instinctively continues to flow with the colonels moves, keeping his tracking, his focus point just above the top of the colonel's hairline at "the spot." Mike's training emphasizes becoming one with the rifle. Mike has achieved that feeling, that sense. He is one with the rifle. He knows if his alignment is on (and he knows that it will be) with this portion of slight aiming adjustment for elevation, the bullet will drop to right where he wants it to impact or very close. He is aiming for mid head. *Hold firm*, he thinks. *Steady.*

Mike has confidence that this aiming adjustment will put the arriving round within a five-inch circle of his intended point of contact. He is consistent now with impact patterns that tight. A round landing two and a half inches above mid head is top of head. Two and a half inches down is chin or neck. All fatal.

Gentle on the trigger; wait for the pause in movement. As with any assignment, a momentary pause in motion or better yet a stationary head would further minimize the chance of a miss.

Breathe in; breathe half out.

The colonel who has killed many Americans, the colonel who will undoubtedly order killings of many more, turns now to yell harshly at a nearby sentry. He stops spinning as he stares and barks at the poor trooper with a disapproving, disgusted frown and glare.

Move with him; one with the rifle; smooth pause.

Hold firm, steady squeeze.

Blam. The weapon discharges and recoils.

The shot streaks, flying toward the colonel's head at three thousand feet per second.

Mike and Jonathan watch each flickering moment, as frame by frame, the round flies. *Watch.*

The bullet impacts face on at the cheek, eye level. *Perfect.*

The face implodes, the head violently jerks, a red stream erupts from the backside as blood, brains, and skull splatter.

Instantly, death. All motor systems, all control, everything living is dead. The corpse abruptly, awkwardly in the unnatural way of death collapses.

The NVA colonel no longer exists. He will kill no more.

Mike and Jonathan, having each seen the impact and the crumpling of the body, turn to lock proud and battle-weary eyes. They feel great relief and immense satisfaction at their success and yet at the same time are viciously repulsed by the savage violence they have watched being unleashed by their hands. Still, they nod approvingly to each other as they exchange a thumbs-up over grimacing grins. Maybe less kids will die. The colonel will kill no more. Hoorah!

FINAL MISSION PART TWO

The startled enemy sentries jump, gasp, and stare. Some of them, the ones closer in, rush to the body. As they move, their heads spin, twist, and swivel, their eyes darting in every direction. In their fear and instant panic, they frantically scan right and left, searching for the source of the shot. Some of the other guards, hoping to encourage the killer to scurry away, randomly spray bullets in the direction they believe best. None of them know where the shot came from.

The instant collapse followed by the crack of this single round interrupting the morning quiet was such a shock, so abrupt, so isolated the guards are powerless. It came out of somewhere and nowhere. The guards saw no movement. There is no enemy presence. All they saw was the gruesome blast to the colonels' head, his brains flying out, and his instantly dead body collapsing, now crumpled and bleeding before them. Dead. They have no clue that two Marines are 680 yards out somewhere in front of them.

The guards do know that someone deadly, someone lethal, is close by but they have no idea where this someone might be. Having seen the colonel, they are not enthused about striking out or randomly searching for their enemy. Heck, at this distance, if the Marines were standing up waving their arms and the guards were looking in the same direction, they'd still be hard to see. Even the dogs are no help; they've been spooked by the random gunfire, the agitation of their masters, and the overall state of disruption and confusion.

Jonathan turns again to give Mike another half-smile and a thumbs-up as he shakes his head, marveling at the precision. He mouths, "Good shot. Hoorah!" They are both relieved at the mission's success.

After waiting several long moments, patiently watching the guards, and seeing no active, direct pursuit coming their way, Mike gives the signal, and slowly, silently, the two Marines gather and stow all their gear and start the slow crawl back toward the jungle.

Once into the shelter of higher grasses, trees, and brush, they stand, peel off and stow their Ghillie suits, grab a quick swallow, retrieve their boonie hats, and begin moving east and toward extraction. As the distance increases and the possibility of their noise being heard decreases, they begin to run toward safety and their escape. *Let's get the heck out of here!*

They are in a full run now, Rogers chasing closely after Smith.

Smith feels a tug at his boot before he sees the tripwire and immediately nosedives for the deck, just as he had been taught in training.

Rogers keeps coming in his shadow but either doesn't have time to dive or doesn't see Smith going down.

The grenade of the booby trap that is flung from the LAWS rocket tube rolls out in front of their path, their movement taking them closer to the coming blast.

Baroom! It explodes in its blast.

Both Marines recoil and collapse, their bodies torn and penetrated by the grenade's shrapnel.

"Oh shit, I'm hit!" Jonathan blurts out, groaning in pain. "I'm really hit."

Both Mike and Jonathan are seriously wounded. Plus, the blast of the grenade's explosion was just that, a profound explosion. The sounds of the eruption might have alerted their pursuers. If they heard it, they're coming. If they are coming, they might be coming in force and bringing those vicious, angry dogs with them.

Mike, a step ahead in the run, is in bad shape. His left knee and leg are torn, bleeding, and nearly gone. Some shrapnel went through the knee; some is embedded. He feels intense pain below the knee. Blood runs down his leg. His boot is on, but he can't flex. His foot dangles.

Jonathan though took much more of the brunt of the blast, in part because he didn't see it coming. He didn't dive. He was still running toward it and upright. The blast of white-hot shrapnel caught his torso and belly full on. He's punctured all up and down his left side, ripped open, and bleeding. Heavily.

Jonathan's wounds have him in major pain. He is doubled up in a fetal position on the ground. He is containing his hurt, fighting off the desire to cry out, doing his best to stay in control and silent. There are numerous, random wounds to his body where the fragments penetrated his flesh, mostly from midthigh up to his chest. Each one is about the size of a kitchen paring knife's blade. There are some tiny slivers and some larger fragments of shrapnel, some the size of a pea, some more like a grape. Jonathan's body caught a bunch of those flying metal blades the grenade blasted, each cutting him wherever they struck. It's bad.

He is bloody and bleeding from many of these wounds. From some, it just flows. Blood is all across his side. His internal injuries may be substantial, who knows. Maybe he has severed veins or arteries. Maybe penetrated intestines. There's no way to know what damage there may be as they lie here in the jungle. He needs medical aid. His wounds are serious, and he is in very severe pain. He needs help.

Mike, seeing the gravity of the wounds, immediately says, "I'm sorry, I'm sorry. Jonathan, I'm so sorry," partly for the severity of the wounds and partly because, as the leader, he takes responsibility. Mostly because it's Jonathan and that it is seriously, maybe even deadly, bad. He got the worst of it.

Both men are in shock. Both are a mess. Mike instantly knows now whatever happens it's going to be all on him.

Belly wounds are intensely painful. Jonathan is doubling up, doing his best like a champ to stay quiet. His pain is too much. He's on it but just barely and is clearly in serious hurt. More moans and cries leak out as he works at bucking up.

Sound betrays snipers. They must be silent to survive. The enemy is nearby and may be coming.

Mike sees that something must be done. Jonathan is suffering. *I've got to reduce the pain.*

Mike lies in the grass next to Jonathan, cupping his mouth, muffling the moans. He pulls out one of the two morphine syrettes he's carrying in his suspenders. He injects Jonathan right at the base of the neck just above his collar. It's the most accessible spot. Jonathan calms a bit.

Marines carry medical gear for themselves. It's routine. You carry what you may want or need if you're the one that's hit. All of what you carry is optional; you can leave it behind to carry more ammo, more water, more whatever, or you can opt for less weight. Just know, if it is you, what you are carrying is what there is. Most carry just what Mike and Jonathan carry on this assignment: a large field bandage, sulfa powder, and two syrettes of morphine. They've never needed them before. They do now. They need what they are carrying and could use having more. *I hope it's enough.*

Mike begins tending to his own left knee. He pulls his belt from his waist, wraps it around his left thigh, pulling tight to make a tourniquet to slow his bleeding. He hopes that the morphine he gave Jonathan will take effect and be enough to let him quiet down.

Jonathan, although somewhat subdued, is still suffering, moaning, and doubling up. He is still in intense pain on intense pain. "I hurt, I hurt. I'm sorry, I hurt."

Enough time has gone by to see that one won't be enough; Mike injects his second syrette. Jonathan settles down, then eyes rolling back, passes out.

Mike opens Jonathan's shirt and unbuttons his pants to get a full view of the damage. Blood is flowing. He shakes sulfa powder from its pouch in wide sweeps onto Jonathan's wounds. Sulfa reduces infection and helps the blood clot.

They each carry a large field bandage, a 6 x 8 gauze pad. Mike folds them out trying to stretch the coverage and applies both his and Jonathan's to the areas of most bleeding as best he can, tying the dressings around with the built-in straps. There are more wounds than bandages. He closes Jonathan's shirt and pants, wrapping him around the middle with his own poncho. He pulls the poncho as tight as he can in his own pain and working at it with the two of them lying in the grass. He wants pressure on Jonathan's wounds. *Got to reduce the bleeding!*

Mike knows he can't walk. With the wounds to his knee, he can't even stand.

Jonathan is out. Even when he comes to, Jonathan won't be walking.

Mike knows he can't leave Jonathan behind. Cannot do it.

If we stay here, we'll be caught. If caught, we'll be tortured and killed.

If I leave Jonathan here alone, he's dead. He'll either lie here, bleed out, and die from these wounds or be found and killed.

He listens intently with adrenaline-alerted nerves and ears for the sounds of sentries or dogs while his mind races with how to reach the extraction point. It's almost four clicks away.

Mike is five feet ten, about 165 pounds. Jonathan is a bit smaller, five eight and 135. *It's good he's a little guy.*

Mike decides he'll load Jonathan onto his back. *I'll get you out!*

Mike's left leg can't even support him. Neither man can walk.

The voice inside says, *Okay, if I can't walk, I'll crawl. Jonathan is seriously wounded, and now with his pain and the morphine he needed, he's out. I won't leave him! I will carry him! I can do it! We can do it!*

I have to! There is no other way. There is no one else. It's Jonathan. He's my responsibility. I'm here, I've got to crawl to get out! He's coming with me! It's my duty. I'm doing it! He worked at convincing himself.

He'll crawl with Jonathan on his back. It's a long crawl.

All Mike knows is he will. *I'm doing it! Is there any choice? We're not staying here!*

He will carry Jonathan on his back, and he'll get to the extraction point in time.

He knows they both are carrying a weapon, ammo, and all their gear.

Yes, he will carry out all those pounds, too. Probably thirty or so pounds for each of them.

Mike is also carrying a green smoke grenade for use at the extraction point to signal and bring in the chopper. Jonathan has the spotter's scope.

Mike, having already used his own, grabs Jonathan's two morphine syrettes out of his vest to have them at the ready for probable use later.

For now, Mike passes on using any morphine himself. First off, yes, he's in pain, deep pain, but he needs to be awake. Besides, he wants to save the last two for Jonathan. When he comes to in a few hours, he will need more relief. *Man, it's a long way through this jungle to our rescue. He's bad, much worse than me. He'll need these!*

It's going to take some time to get to the LZ. *Jonathan is bad and in big trouble. We need help. I'm the one still awake, still moving. I've going to do this! For now, just grin and crawl with that pain. No morphine for me. I'm okay. He's going to need more. We're doing this!*

Mike unloads and clears both rifles, stashing the loaded magazines he removes into his vest. *I might need these later.* Using a bootlace, he ties the flash suppresser of Jonathan's weapon to Jonathan's right boot. It will drag nose first behind them. He does the same with his own weapon, tying it to his good leg's right boot. Both rifles will drag behind.

Mike stows the bandage wrappings, the paper, and the empty syrettes inside one of the bags. Now, he has everything they brought with them. *We leave no evidence of our presence or our exit behind. We weren't here.*

Except this time, Mike, crawling with Jonathan on his back, will leave something behind. The scrapes on their path of the dragging rifles. The impressions of his belly left on the grass and in the mud by the weight of their two bodies, one crawling carrying the other. They are both bleeding, leaving their blood on the trail. Still, Mike can't even conceive the thought of leaving any of their gear behind besides that trail of blood. He wants it all, just in case. He may yet need as much firepower as possible.

It's all coming with us! He had been trained. *We don't leave anything behind.*

If we get caught on our way out, I've got my .45 on my waist, my K bar on my shoulder, and magazines of ammo in my vest. Good Lord, give me a chance to reel in my rifle!

Finally, Mike uses his own poncho to wrap Jonathan to his back. He pulls the sleeves under his belly and ties them together tightly around his chest. Mike knows he will need to balance Jonathan's weight. *Got to have him securely on my back. Okay, Buddy, are you about ready? Here we go, hoorah!*

Mike estimates there are something like three clicks or a bit more to the extraction LZ and safety. He knows it may be four, but it helps him for now to think it's less.

With Jonathan on his back, Mike can't lift his own body. Instead, using his shoulders, back, elbows, and his good right leg and knee, he slides his body forward on the grass, scooching along at about six to sometimes as much as eight inches.

He stops and lifts his head off the deck to listen. Jonathan is breathing. No other sounds besides the birds and the wind. *Good. So far, safe.*

Mike checks his compass, picks a landmark to crawl toward, and starts. He knows if he goes east toward South Vietnam, even if they don't make it exactly to the drop LZ, they will have a chance. *Got to get us through the jungle and into a clearing. Then we will have the chance of being found. They will be there. We're doing it!*

Mike does the best he can with a man on his back, all the gear, and dragging their weapons. He tries in vain to avoid putting pressure on his wounded left leg. Mike twists and worms forward inch by inch, stifling any moans along the way.

He knows the horror NVA soldiers have done to captured snipers. Too many of the stories had been told.

About one in four of the Marines operating as scout/sniper, 0317 MOS (Military Occupational Specialty), never come home.

Those poor slugs were killed. Dead.

The ones that were captured were beaten, often enduring vicious cuttings and torture before death. NVA soldiers are fond of using knives to inflict pain and torment on their captives. Some of the bodies had been found naked, beaten, and lashed to crossed fence beams. Their faces and torsos bore cuts with slices up and down, right and left. Bellies had been sliced open, and warm intestines, looking like giant gray slimy tube worms, were pulled from the open bloody stomach wound and fed to grunting village piglets. All while the terrified victim was just barely breathing, just barely alive. Sex organs were often removed.

There would be no rescue, only slow certain, horrid terror and pain before the relief of death. Then dead forever.

No captured Marine sniper was ever a POW.

In fact, officially there are no Marines in Laos, allowing no room for those captured to survive. For this assignment, they wear no dog tags, no stripes, no insignia of any kind. They are not identifiable as US Marines. Except by everything they are and everything they do. All the enemy will leave behind if they fail is their bodies. Or pieces of their bodies.

There is no stopping! We are going to make it!

It's well beyond 1100 hours (11:00 a.m.), the first of three prearranged times that a chopper will be at the pickup LZ looking for them.

There is another at 1400 (2:00 p.m.). And a final at 1700 (5:00 p.m.).

These are the extraction times for this assignment. The only extraction times.

Miss making extraction, and the odds of surviving undetected with these wounds are slim.

That's just another way to dead. Forget it! Jonathan, we will get there! We are doing this!

Off in the distance, he hears scattered gunfire.

Could that be the guards trailing us? No, that sounds far enough away. We're safe! We keep going!

Pulling his right knee up, shifting elbows forward, balancing Jonathan between his shoulders, Mike never stops moving.

He develops a rhythm. Elbow, knee, elbow. He sets a pace. Just like in training on those forced marches. *Set a pace. We keep going! We don't stop!*

The jungle provides some shade, but soon the constant effort, the wounds, the blood loss, and the subsiding blessing of shock bring heat, pain, and exhaustion.

Still, there's the ever-present dark fears of capture, torture, and death; the duty to get Jonathan out; the serious nature of his wounds; and the determination to make that final extraction time.

Mike hears S/Sgt. Henry, his drill instructor, telling him, "You can do this. Marines don't quit. Marines don't leave another Marine.

"You are a part of the finest fighting force on the planet.

"Your training has prepared you. Follow your training, never stop."

Mike remembers S/Sgt. Henry: "God created the Marine Corps to save America so Americans could worship God."

He remembers a chapel service where the priest gave last rites, telling them, "If you get in trouble in Vietnam, your soul will be safe."

Even though his conversations with God were already frequent before Vietnam, now ever since meeting S/Sgt. Henry and seeing his deep, profound personal faith, Mike has begun revving up his prayer talk. Every day in Vietnam, Mike and the Lord have frequent, nearly constant conversations.

Hey, consider this. Here's how it is.

Mike is in Vietnam, carrying a rifle at war. He is out in the jungle hunting enemy troops over half of the time. He is totally alone or has just his spotter for backup if they are ever detected. He has no radio to call for help. He is pursuing the enemy either to observe or to hunt a specific individual. Both activities require him to be in direct contact. When he is successful, he is hiding within a few hundred yards of fully armed NVA soldiers. He sees them. They are hunting Americans. They are hunting him. He is their invisible prey. They are eager to find him and when they do to kill him.

He is a loner and thrives on being alone. He likes the hunt. He has had a long, enduring faith for many years and finds comfort and strength in it. Having this great relationship and frequent conversations with God is a good idea.

This time the conversation starts with *Heavenly Father* (that's how Mike's mom always began), *help us. Give me strength. Help me, Lord! Keep me going!*

Mike talks with himself and God constantly, working at keeping the communication lines open. He wants to ensure his pleas are consistent enough to be heard. The activity of praying helps him stay in motion. It gives him something to focus on besides his pain, the scraping along in the grass, and the weight and burden of his wounded spotter. It helps to calm his soul. To give him peace. *His yoke is light!*

Jonathan, stay with me! Jonathan, we'll make it, we don't quit! Please don't quit!

Mike is seeking the strength and energy to continue. He wants and needs God's help.

Mike pushes forward, up the grade. *Keep moving! We are doing this!*

He never considers quitting. He knows his hero, Gunnery Sergeant Carlos Hathcock, faced many difficult missions and never quit.

Elbow, knee, elbow. *Keep going! Dear God, help us!*

They come to an area of wetter jungle. The water soaks his belly, his elbows, his knees. It is welcomed, cool relief.

Mike rolls Jonathan off his back and onto the ground beside him. Jonathan's belly is oozing blood but much slower than before. He's breathing and beginning to groan. Mike wants to curb the bleeding.

He digs down in the thick mud with his knife and his hands scooping and packing Jonathan's belly wounds with it as best he can.

Then taking his knife after wiping the blade, Mike cuts the sleeves from Jonathan's utilities then from his own. Jonathan needs more bandages. He uses the strips of green utility cloth to fashion another improvised band of bindings. Blood is everywhere but less than before. It doesn't look good. *The mud will help.*

Mike takes a sip from his canteen and carefully pours a few drops of water into Jonathan's mouth. *We need it! Take a little sip. We're doing this!*

Seeing agony on his face, Mike gives Jonathan one of the remaining morphine shots. He whispers more words of encouragement. "Buck up, Marine! Come on, man! We'll get there! We will! We don't quit! Hoorah!"

It's a pleading phrase Mike repeats throughout the crawl. To himself on the inside: *Oh please, Jonathan, hang in there. I'm so sorry!*

It's after the 1400 extraction time. Only one more chance remains. He has crawled and crawled. There is still more crawling to do.

"Dear God, give me strength." Keep going!

At this pace, crawling inches with a badly wounded Jonathan on his back, Mike knows there's still a considerable distance to go. He moves with care to balance Jonathan's weight, using his shoulder blades, elbows, and back muscles, trying to ignore the pain.

Got to get to the landing zone! I'm not leaving you behind! We're doing this!

Mike keeps crawling, his elbows now feeling raw. His functioning right leg and knee are scraped, bruised, and aching.

It's nearly 1700 now. He's got to move faster, got to get there. *Rescue is coming. We can't miss getting there or we'll die!*

Elbow, knee, elbow. Mike in the final stretch is doing a sprint to the zone now, panicking that time is running out.

Reaching a clearing, Mike stops, lays his face down, and listens. Jonathan is quiet on his back.

First, there's nothing to hear. He listens again, harder.

Wait, is that a distant rotor beat? He grabs for the smoke.

Now, hearing that the beat is a little louder, Mike pulls the pin on the green smoke and the best he can while lying on the ground, he flings it.

The Huey turns to the smoke, diving for the LZ, coming almost straight in.

Thank you, Jesus! Mike stops moving to stare as the Huey, now their rescuing angel, approaches and begins to descend.

Huh, look at that. What's this? That's weird. That's not right.

Choppers always make a once-around clearing circle of a LZ to draw out any hidden enemy fire before committing to a landing. It's one of their consistent safety routines. But this time, this crew, even though they're out here in no-man's-land, comes right in. No circling. Just straight in.

What? Why are they risking this expedited, straight in landing maneuver?

Mike never knows why. Most likely, they're a bit frantic in their search for their missing sniper team. They know that they are the teams' final chance. Their last hope.

As Mike watches, the approaching chopper descends and then flares, the nose coming up as the pilot slows airspeed and cushions the landing.

On the underbelly, the name "Katye" is painted in scrolling white lettering between the skids. Crews would sometimes add names for a touch of home or of a love left behind. Maybe Katye was the skipper's girl, maybe his daughter.

Everyone who saw the name had a momentary thought for the girl I left behind. Or of the one I don't really know, but even without knowing, she's on my mind. If she knew me, maybe she'd be waiting.

Mike lays his face back down in the grass, with Jonathan still strapped to his back. He's too wasted now to even push Jonathan off. He closes his eyes against the cool rotor blast and sighs in relief. *Sweet Jesus, thank God they're here! Thank you, Jesus! Jonathan, they're here!*

As soon as the chopper turned, Mike was ecstatic in his relief.

And just as suddenly he had begun feeling intense, overwhelming nauseous pain. Up to now, he had focused everything on getting here, on keeping moving. His pain had waited. No more.

Now, his back, arms, elbows, his bruised and scraped good knee, and especially his wounded leg and knee—it all screeches. He lies spent in the dirt.

The corpsman and crew chief come running to Mike and Jonathan.

Smith can hardly lift his head as he points to Rogers, telling the corpsman, "Him first! He needs you! Take care of Jonathan! Please!"

The corpsman pulls Jonathan off Mike's back, gently unfolding the poncho to get a good look. His eyes go soft as he turns back.

He shakes his head, moving from Jonathan to tend to Mike.

"I'm sorry. He's gone. He didn't make it."

Mike's head spins. "Wait, what? No, check again! He was alive! I checked! It can't be."

He had checked Jonathan all along the way, about once each hour. He was alive. This last time maybe a bit more. *He can't be dead! He can't be! No!*

The corpsman rolls Mike over, releases the tourniquet above his knee, freshens the dressing, pops morphine into Mike's thigh, and says, "You're good. You're safe. We're going to get you home.

"Your knee looks like it's a mess, but we're heading back to base in just a couple of minutes. We'll land right at the medevac hot spot; docs'll be there to meet us. You'll go right in to medical. I don't know; you might lose the leg. But those guys are good; could be they may save it. But, man, you're safe. We'll get you both back. We found you. You made it."

Mike: "But are you sure? Really sure? He was alive!"

Corpsman: "Yes. I'm sorry. Yes, I'm sure."

Mike is stunned.

Corpsman: "You did all you could."

The one that survived has a blown-up left knee with blood staining his dragging limb. He has blood soaking his back and legs from his wounds and the wounds of his spotter. His shock and adrenaline have kept him going, but now he can barely lift his head. His elbows are raw, his trousers worn through on the good leg, his belly a mixture of sweat, blood, grime, and muddy grass stains from sliding his way here. His eyes flicker, darting from side to side as they search the horizon.

He's trying to believe the lying corpsman. He has a frantic, drawn, deeply pained, and empty gaze. A gaze like you sometimes will see on those much older men who have lived a life with all the pain it can bring. He's completely, totally worn out and exhausted. Spent. Maybe saved. Maybe safe.

The corpsman leaves Mike for a moment to join the crew chief who has been attending to Jonathan. For several moments, they prepare the body for transport, carefully positioning and then wrapping Jonathan in his poncho.

The two of them lift, carry, and load Pfc. Jonathan Rogers's body onto Katye. They do it with reverence, care, honor, and respect.

They lash him securely to the deck.

All five Americans present have seen portions of this evolution and know they are in the presence of the death of a brother. Each one feels a painful ache in his heart.

For Mike, it's intense and very personal. This was Jonathan. His pain is eye watering and throat-aching. He is nauseous but too exhausted and too famished to barf. It's the empty, sour-in-the-pit-of-your-stomach overwhelming, impossible-to-speak grief. *Jonathan!*

His swollen eyes and streaming tears say, "*Don't even think about trying to talk to me. Not now. I need a few alone minutes. Just leave me alone!*"

It hurts the way only a death of one you love hurts. Even when you didn't mean to.

A brother's dead. Jonathan is dead. It can't be true. It's true: he's dead.

Poor, dead young Jonathan, wrapped now in that poncho, is one of them, just a few short hours ago alive.

May God rest his soul.

The crew chief and corpsman come back to lift the limp, grimacing, and spent Corporal Michael T. Smith onto a web seat for the flight back to base.

Mike is embarrassed and a bit self-conscious to be moaning, but it's just impossible to stay quiet. He urgently cries out in his newfound pain. The corpsman gives him another, smaller shot while starting an IV. He leans in to offer Mike some words of comfort, saying, "I saw what you did for your buddy. Amazing. You did more than just get here. The bandages. The strips you cut off of your shirts. The mud. Man, you did all you could with what you had. I couldn't have done better."

Mike nods while on the inside asking himself, *Yeah, but why did he have to die? Why?*

Unbelievable. *Jonathan, I'm so sorry!*

A canteen is passed. It's Mike's first water in several hours. He lifts his face taking a long draw. Tears continue to stream. The aircrew focuses on their duties and turn their eyes away.

Dead.

As the Huey lifts and starts its acceleration, the nose leans forward, the rotor blades increase their bite, and the airspeed climbs. The crew has a wounded Marine on board. This is an urgent extraction. They will be flying home at max speed. The pilot pulls strong on the collective, rolling the nose further down, tilting the rotors toward home. They gain speed, going all out for the airfield back at the base.

With the lean of the airframe now tilting the Huey forward, Mike feels himself leaning chest first nearly too far forward. He tries to keep from rolling over in the seat like some kind of spaz by pushing back against the floor as hard as he can muster with his one good leg just trying his best to stay put. He feels the tilt trying to dump him on his face. The pressure he can muster in his petered-out state is pathetic. He's a wet noodle. Wimpy. A wuss. No one notices his struggle.

These amazing pilots that drove this angel helicopter out here to come searching for him and his green smoke don't even realize they're making his lifesaving rescue ride to safety in these few moments a tiny measure of hell. Their effort at a speedy extraction is about to dump him on his nose. Geez, it's nothing like what he just endured, but it's still kind of annoying. He hides his frustration inside, and grumbles to himself, *Airwing.* Grunts often wonder about airwing Marines. At the same time, it feels incredibly, wonderfully safe and such a sweet relief to be back with Marines. *Even if they are airwing*

Marines, they're Marines. Hoorah! I'm safe. On the way home. Almost. These guys are hotdogs! Our hotdogs!

Somehow it feels slightly better in the moment to have something inside to bitch about. *Jonathan!*

Now that he's riding, there is exhaustion, pain, and overwhelming relief to accompany his grief. He is safe.

But inside, from now on and forever more, there is with him this underlying constant, a deep nagging grief. His new constant, permanent partner and shadow. *Jonathan is dead. Unbelievable!*

Inside, he prays again. *Dear God, thank you. Thank you for this. I knew we'd get here. I wanted to get him help. Thanks for sending them to find us. Be with Jonathan now, Lord. Welcome him to You. I tried to save him. Why Jonathan? Why him? I'm sorry, Jonathan, so sorry! Why?*

As the aircraft reaches cruising speed, the ride levels out. Mike's no longer falling out.

The Huey is streaking along at fifteen hundred feet, 110 or better knots, beating feet back to base. Watching as the landscape slips by lickety-split, feeling the rush of low-level flight, Mike thinks to himself, *Man, these Airedales really do have it made.* He closes his eyes. Doped and exhausted, he's soon passed out or asleep.

The pilot radios ahead, "Lima November One Six crossing X-ray inbound for Mike Spot 1 with one KIA, one WIA, fifteen minutes out, over."

At touchdown, a running team of corpsmen and doctors rush in to pull wounded, limp, and sedated Corporal Smith from Katye; they plop him onto a waiting stretcher and dash him and his torn leg into field surgery.

There is no goodbye.

Mike never sees Jonathan again.

After the Mission— Bronze Star Forty-Four Years Later

The surgical team at the field hospital just off the medivac helicopter pad works on Mike's leg. He is in surgery there for several hours, receiving treatment, blood, medications, and IVs.

Within seventy-two hours, Mike is on a medevac aircraft out of Vietnam and home to Balboa Naval Hospital in San Diego, where he has three additional surgeries. The first occurs within hours of his arrival. He sleeps while enroute and for several days after.

Mike's final mission was in January 1970. His surgeries, the recovery, and rehab while at Balboa last just over four months. His release from Balboa back to Camp Pendleton is a week, maybe two, before his discharge.

He calls home and speaks with his wife about three months into his recovery. He didn't call her earlier. He didn't want her to see him until he was cleaned up and looked better. When he calls, she learns he was wounded and is safe. He's home.

He doesn't call his parents until he has been discharged from the hospital, well on the road to recovery, and is back at Camp Pendleton. He didn't want to upset his mom. He knew his dad could take any hard news, but Mike says, "My mom, I didn't want to stress her."

Mike: "When I finally did talk to my father, it was after I was back at Pendleton. I said, 'Yeah, I was wounded. I've had surgery on my leg. All's better now.'"

Phil: "Did your dad know what you did? Did he know what you had gone through?"

Mike: "He knew I was a scout/sniper. We never spoke about what I did. He died before we were at a place where we could talk about it. Mom never knew. He died when I was in my thirties, mid-1980s. When he passed, he and my mom died forty-five days apart. They'd been married forty-five years. My dad was a heavy smoker and, as I have mentioned, a heavy drinker. He ended up having open-heart surgery in our local hospital. I had gone to the hospital to visit my dad.

"When I got home, our associate pastor was in our living room. My mind goes, 'Dad couldn't have died that fast.' My wife says, 'Pastor Skip is here because your mom died a little while ago.'

"I say, 'Oh?'

"My sister had brought my mom to see Dad earlier that day and was on the way home with her when Mom laid her head back on the car seat like she was going to take a nap. That was it. When they drove into town, my sister went straight to the hospital. They pronounced her dead. That was like forty-five days before Dad died.

"To this day, I show very little emotion because I'd seen my father. When his parents died, when his close friends died, my father never showed emotion. I thought that was the way it's supposed to be. When my son died, I just couldn't show emotion; I didn't know how."

Phil: "Did your father ever say, 'I love you' to you?"

Mike: "I don't remember him saying that. I don't ever remember him saying that. I took Pastor Vernon to see my dad when he was in the hospital. He grabbed Pastor Vernon's hand. 'What do I have to do to be with Mable?' He wanted to know how to be in heaven with my mom. I didn't expect that. That was a curve."

Phil: "Do you think he was making peace with God?"

Mike: "Oh yeah, my mom was a Baptist Christian. She buried her religion as much as she could around my father. As kids, we went to church just a few times. Just with her. He'd be out hunting somewhere. Later, as I grew up, he'd let me skip church and even school to go hunting with him."

Mike: "Many, many years later I had some business at Mare Island Naval Shipyard in Vallejo. It's like forty some years later. I'm working for an insurance company. My job was to help teach truckers about safety. Some of the trucks were on the base. I'm on my way in to check these trucks, these crews. Just a normal, routine visit. The officer at the check-in gate who looks at my Marine Corps credentials, he's a junior, one-bar navy officer, maybe an ensign, maybe lieutenant JG (Junior Grade). Anyway, he looks me up on a screen. 'It says here you were awarded the Bronze Star.'

"I'm like, 'Pardon, me? It does? I never received a Bronze Star.'

"His name might have been Johnson. He was kinda tall, red hair, and very fair-skinned like a typical redhead. He turns back to his screen, reads a bit more, and says, 'We can take care of that.'

"Pretty quick, maybe two weeks later, I get in the mail the medal and the certificate. It's dated the fifth day of April 2014, which was about two weeks after that conversation at the gate. I had no idea all those years. Forty-four years."

The certificate reads:

THE UNITED STATES OF AMERICA
THIS IS TO CERTIFY THAT
THE PRESIDENT OF THE UNITED STATES OF AMERICA
HAS AWARDED THE
BRONZE STAR MEDAL
WITH COMBAT "V"
TO
CORPORAL MICHAEL T. SMITH, UNITED STATES MARINE CORPS
FOR
SERVICE IN THE REPUBLIC OF VIETNAM ON 18 JANUARY 1970
GIVEN THIS 5TH DAY OF APRIL 2014 PAUL R. IGNATUS, SECRETARY OF THE NAVY

Mike: "The date on the citation in January 1970 is a bit after when Jonathan and I went in. It's more likely a date when I was already back at Balboa but must be for what had happened to us. Maybe it was dated forward a bit to avoid direct connection with being in Laos. I don't know. Maybe it had something to do with when the write-up was done. Who knows? Shoot, it's so many years later. I was amazed. Interesting too that it is only listed as signed and dated when it is actually issued and bears the signature of the guy that was Secretary of the Navy back in those years, not the 2014 guy. I'd been around bases and at the VA lots of times. No one before had said anything about a Bronze Star."

"When it came, it was just the certificate and a really classy, blue flip-top display box with the medal and ribbons hanging inside on a white silky looking lining. No narrative of the award came with it. Sometimes they will use the write-up that was submitted in the application for the award to create a narrative of what had happened. Many times, the narrative is read at the presentation ceremony. If presented in the field, there would have been a formal ceremony with formations, salutes, and pinning. I have stood in many such ceremonies in my time."

"It's forty-four years later. I'm sixty-five. A long time and a long way from active duty. A long way from Vietnam. A long time from what happened. No unit to stand with. There is no ceremony. No presentation. No narrative. Just an envelope in the mail. Perhaps because we weren't in Laos. I don't know. Just the certificate and the medal. It is something to see. Seems like all these years the award was out there waiting to be claimed; I just never knew it.

"I have the box the medal came in in my living room on top of a dresser. It's open where I can see it. I'm glad to have it. No one knows I have it except me. That's just fine with me.

"Even though it's forty-four years later, it's good to have it. One of the guys that picked us up that day took the time to write us up. It went through the process and was approved. Somehow, no notice had ever gotten to me.

"I tried to do all I could. I wish Jonathan was alive. Every day, I wish Jonathan was alive."

FINAL CONVERSATION—IT WASN'T YOU

Authors Note: This is the final of several conversations Mike and I had while we worked on gathering the details of his story. Other conversations follow. Look for the note ahead explaining our process.

Phil: "Let's talk a bit more about what happened on the final mission. That grenade got Jonathan big time. It had to be awful."

Mike: "It was. That's where my guilt has riddled me for so many years. When I felt the trip wire, I knew it was trouble."

Phil: "It had to go all up and down his frame."

Mike: "Mostly from midthigh up."

Phil: "What happens to his clothes when the grenade hits?"

Mike: "It shreds them and pulls fabric into the wounds."

Phil: "You've got to have a bloody mess there. And a lot of ugly tears to his body, right? It's got to be bad."

Mike: "And that's why it's been so hard."

Phil: "He had to be doubling over."

Mike: "He was balled up in the fetal position on the ground."

Phil: "And writhing in pain?"

Mike: "Yeah. But he was doing a good job of containing the pain."

Phil: "He had to be crying out."

Mike: "No, he knew we had to be quiet. He was swallowing it, keeping it inside. You could tell he needed help. That's why I gave him my morphine right away, to calm him down. Then I'm trying to roll him over and get him to open his fetal ball to get a look, to access his wounds. I say, 'Jonathan, I've got to see how bad this is.' There were ten to twelve places, mostly in his abdomen along the left side of his body. He was all chewed up. Bloody and bleeding. It wouldn't do much good to wipe at it. Blood was coming and would just keep coming. I grabbed the sulfa powder; it helps the bleeding subside. It causes the blood to coagulate. I sprinkled it all along his wounds."

Phil: "You are both carrying sulfa powder, so you used both of them?"

Mike: "I used his first and then mine. Then I put two bandages with the long ties…"

Phil: "Those were 4 x 6?"

Mike: "No, more like 6 x 8. I put the two of those on. For a while, it appeared to work. And then he was, 'I hurt, I hurt, I hurt! I'm sorry, I hurt.' He was saying, 'I'm sorry' because in his pain, he just couldn't stop moaning and groaning out loud. Our rules are no noise. Noise brings death. So, I gave him the second morphine. My last dose of morphine. Then he settled down and was pretty much out of it."

Phil: "He wasn't conscious anymore, right?"

Mike: "His eyes were rolled back. He was breathing. He wasn't moaning anymore.

"I took his uniform and didn't put it back on but kind of wrapped it around for further compression and then wrapped him in his poncho, folding it in so his belt coming around it held it all together. Then I tended to my knee."

Phil: "Anything hit his face?"

Mike: "No."

Phil: "Jonathan was twenty?"

Mike: "Maybe nineteen; I think I was a bit ahead of him. I was twenty-one a couple weeks before in December. I'm not sure about him. We never asked that kind of question, and I never looked at his dog tags."

Phil: "Did you guys eat together? Play cards together?"

Mike: "No, but sometimes we would eat our special diet together but not very often. His sleep schedule was different than mine, and the two of us weren't sleeping in the same part of the camp. They had us spread around with none of us too close to another guy, so we weren't clustered up in case of mortars. No, we never played cards."

Phil: "You're a real loner kind of guy."

Mike: "I was taught to be that way by Carlos because it's hard to lose somebody. You get to know them. You get to be friends. You like each other. Then if they get killed, your grief and grieving will mess up your judgment. Because then you want revenge, then you do stupid things. Occasionally, our paths would cross. We would get together and talk about the next assignment. All that we needed to do to prepare, what tactics we were planning, things like that as the next assignment got close."

Phil: "I would assume that after he had seen your performance, he would be like, 'How do you do that?'"

Mike: "He wanted to do that himself. He was studying to be a scout/sniper."

Phil: "Yeah, but your ability to shoot, especially at those distances, is way beyond most people's. You know that, right?"

Mike: "Carlos was a better shot then me."

Phil: "And maybe your dad was a better shot than you, possibly. I mean in his day; your dad was pretty darn good."

Mike: "Oh, my dad was a fabulous shot. But after I got to Vietnam, then I was probably a better shot than him. Things evolve with practice and repetition. Knowledge. Knowing the weapon. Knowing the ammunition. Keep in mind, we were out in the jungle where there are people wanting to find and kill us. We didn't want that to happen. We weren't going to be safe until our tour was up. We are going back out hunting again in a few days right after each completed mission. When we go out, they are hunting us too. The better we were at what we are doing, making one precise shot from a great distance, the less chance we gave them to get us. So, yes, one with the rifle. You have all these things that factor in.

"Back then, we didn't have any fancy handheld calculators or aiming systems. We had Kentucky windage. You know, using your built-in calculator, the one in your head. Your noggin. We were good, maybe a bit better than good at what we were doing just to get into the school. Then when we got into the field and were doing our assignments day after day, we got better. Much better. Seeing the enemy out there carrying rifles, looking for you, wanting to shoot you and if they can kill you will improve a man's focus."

Phil: "Okay, off Katye, they take you right into surgery. Afterward, while you are still in a highly medicated state, they fly you to Balboa. More surgery and finally you come out, wake up, and find yourself in nearly one piece. A day or so before, you spent something like eight or nine hours crawling in the mud on your belly while badly wounded with your worst wounded, bleeding spotter wrapped to you on your back. All your gear. All his gear. Dragging the rifles. You had to be totally beat."

Mike: "I slept for two days."

Phil: "You had to be so tired."

Mike: "Yeah, they had me on IVs. I'd wake up for a few seconds, sort of peek around to see where I was. Was I safe? Pretty quick, my eyes would just go closed. I still couldn't believe it."

Phil: "Were they pumping you with blood?"

Mike: "No, that happened earlier at the field hospital."

Phil: "Because you had been bleeding throughout that day?"

Mike: "Well, I did have it tourniqueted fairly tight. I probably lost two pints while crawling out. I checked the knee each time I checked Jonathan, which was about every hour. I just loosened it enough to let blood go to my foot a little bit at a time. I didn't want to risk losing my leg."

Phil: "Jonathan didn't have a chance to say very much other than, 'I'm hit,' did he?"

Mike: "His first words, were 'Oh, shit!'

"I'm like, 'Jonathan, I'm so sorry!' I was feeling super guilty. Just the way it happened. He was right in; his foot was coming in as my foot was lifting up to hit the spot I just used. We were that close together."

Phil: "Did you tell him to do that?"

Mike: "No, it's just the way we ran."

Phil: "Always?"

Mike: "Always, if we were running, we were that close to each other."

Phil: "Was the jungle so thick that you two felt it was necessary to be that close? He just was concerned that he might lose you, or what do you think it was?"

Mike: "That's just the way he did it, almost running on top of my steps. I never complained."

Phil: "You say, that's the way he did it? Is that right? If he had been, let's say ten paces behind you, he might have seen you dive and had a chance to dive too."

Mike: "Oh, believe me, I have played with that scenario. A million times. Too close, even like five feet behind, maybe even worse. Diving into a grenade...could be head wounds. Worse."

Phil: "Yes, but off to the side or a bit further back, maybe it would have missed him or maybe resulted in less damage done. You found trip wires on other assignments. right?"

Mike: "Yes. I was walking those times."

Phil: "What makes you think you should have found this one?"

Mike: "Just guilt."

Phil: "Did other Marines trigger trip wires?"

Mike: "Yes. There were many guys killed, some wounded."

Phil: "Did you put that trip wire there?"

Mike: "No."

Phil: "That LAWS tube holding that grenade hanging in that tree. Did you put it there?"

Mike: "No."

Phil: "Those guys that put the trip wire booby trap there. Do they have any responsibility on this?

Why are you taking responsibility for what those people put in place that got you and Jonathan wounded?"

Mike: "I was trained on trip wires, and he was my responsibility."

Phil: "You didn't see it, Mike."

Mike: "I know. But you've got to be there to understand. I mean you just, I just..."

Phil: "I'm trying to tell you there is no rational person that would say every trip wire placed as a booby trap can be seen."

Mike: "I've been riddled with guilt from that moment."

Phil: "I hear how you're still carrying so much guilt. It's in you. A ton. You need to get rid of that, man. This, this is an amazingly heroic story. And you are the hero. How far did you carry this man?"

Mike: "Almost four clicks."

Phil: "Okay. So, you can't stand up, right? You can't stand at all. Why didn't you leave some of that crap that was on your back?"

Mike: "I may have needed it. We were trained to carry only what we needed. I wasn't sure if I might need some of it on the way out."

Phil: "And you were trained to be flexible, to change the rules, to do what was needed. To improvise. I can't figure out why you didn't just leave some of it. Bury it. Leave it behind, lighten your load.

You do know you are so, so lucky to have survived? When the grenade goes off, it made a huge explosion, right? You're still not all that far from the mansion where you took the shot. It's amazing they didn't hear it and come running to get you."

Mike: "The good thing is the jungle muffles sound. The growth, the foliage, it sends sound everywhere. That sound is bouncing off the trees, bouncing off the leaves; it's actually partially muffled."

Phil: "Yes, but don't you think if one of them had been within a half a mile, they would have come running?"

Mike: "Well, yes. Exactly."

Phil: "Back to Balboa. You are beyond the couple days of sleeping. You are starting to talk with the people around you. Did you ask what happened?"

Mike: "The first thing that crossed my mind was I want to be the one to notify Jonathan's relatives. I didn't want a Western Union letter going to his whatever."

Phil: "You are realizing he's dead. You are just starting to think and process this through. You're asking these people to help you contact his family. That doesn't work. Who are you talking to about what you have experienced? Are you telling anyone what you have been through?"

Mike: "I pretty much shut up."

Phil: "Didn't some of the nurses ask what had happened?"

Mike: "No, they are trained not to."

Phil: "Is that right?"

Mike: "They were trained to let you talk all you wanted but to not ask specific questions of the wounded. They didn't want to set off traumatic memories or get their patient all riled up.

All these wounded guys, some terribly wounded, were just out of combat. Many of them took what had happened hard. Most of them were much worse than me. At Balboa, I was one of the lucky ones."

Phil: "Did you recognize the guy in the mirror?"

Mike: "My first thought was 'I failed.'"

Phil: "Mike, it's not you. It's not you."

Mike: "Carlos had said, 'Do not get attached. Because if you do and they die, it will haunt you forever.' He spoke from experience. It's one thing to think about. It's another thing to live with."

Phil: "Yeah, this is something you have lived with every day of your life since it happened, but you can't take responsibility for his death. It wasn't you."

Mike: "Maybe. Maybe. I don't listen."

Phil: "Maybe that's why I am here in part, to tell you it wasn't you."

Mike: "I've been waiting for God to tell me that. Maybe one day He will, or maybe you're His messenger."

Phil: "You went back to work with people who knew you. Didn't you talk to them about what you had been through?"

Mike: "No. I went back. I became a workaholic. We never talked about it."

Phil: "I would have found myself maybe one evening out having happy hour at some restaurant or hanging at some bowling alley talking with whoever and going, 'Here's where I have been and here's what happened.' I don't think I could have held it in. But you held it all in. Jonathan had to know how badly he was wounded. He must have realized, 'I'm not going to make it out of here.' A part of you must have thought so too."

Mike: "I was going to do all I could to get him out alive."

Phil: "You did. You did. Mike, you did all you could have. You did more than required. More than expected, and more than many others in the same situation would or could have. It wasn't you."

"It wasn't you, my friend. It wasn't you."

DEDICATION

PRIVATE FIRST CLASS JONATHAN ROGERS
KILLED IN ACTION JANUARY 1970

Jonathan, my Marine brother, and friend, gave his life doing what American Servicemen whether Army, Airforce, Navy, or Marine serve to do. Save lives and preserve freedom.

We served in part to defend our country, to stand beside and with each other, to save innocent lives, and to be a part of bringing a greater freedom to dark places in our world.

Jonathan helped us succeed. Every assignment he was a part of saved others.

Jonathan was the man helping me, the Marine right beside me. He was the guy who had my back.

He was not going to be left behind.

I'm still and always will be carrying him.

Semper Fi! Hoorah!

"For God so loved the world that he gave his one and only Son, that whoever believes in him shall not perish but have eternal life." John 3:16

THANKS AND APPRECIATION

Mike, thank you.

On behalf of Jonathan, every Marine, and all of our readers, thank you for what you did trying to bring that Marine, that brother, that friend, and your own wonderful self to survival and safety.

Thank you for sharing your incredible story. What you did was amazing.

What you did continues to be amazing.

Most of us, even back when we were young and full of muscles and vigor, would have quit the effort of carrying someone that far crawling if we were doing it with two good legs. Your drive, your persistence is impressive. It says something about your commitment to Jonathan. You kept going; you never quit. Pushing through the jungle, over three clicks, moving forward inches at a time with a wounded brother on your back, talking and praying to yourself to keep up the whispering encouragement to him even as he slips quietly away.

You have never used these words, but that passion you showed trying to help Jonathan, all that you did, comes from the love of a brother in need.

When I read what I wrote down, it's one of those stories that puts a lump in my throat and pride in my heart. Amazing. So proud of you.

Thank you.

And to all of you Vietnam vets reading this, thank you too. You all rate a snappy salute, a warm hug, and a big thank you!

Mike, thank you for going on after, for living a life beyond those terrible years. And good on you for coming to find a measure of peace in your soul in the knowledge of God's forgiveness and grace. I see that in who you are.

Now, before you get too big a head, let's confess much credit belongs to the powerful love of your wife and family.

In all your days forward, we ask that God's comfort and peace be with you now and forever. We ask the same for all vets.

Thanks for letting your Marine Corps story come out. It needed out and deserves to be heard. Thank you for feeling safe telling it.

You are a fine man. An outstanding Marine!

Semper Fidelis! Hoorah!

You did everything you could.

We're proud to know you.

It wasn't you.

Peace and love.

Growing Up in Merced— Hunting with Dad

B orn in 1948, Michael Smith grew up a baby boomer in the southern San Joaquin valley of California. This valley is one of the grandest agricultural heartlands of our nation, with a broad diversity of crops, livestock, small ranches, and farms. His hometown, Merced, is the county seat with the nearest major city, Fresno, about fifty miles to the south. Its flat valley land is ideal for nut trees and cattle ranches.

Not far to the east is Yosemite Valley, one of the most glorious natural national parks featuring spectacular granite formations including El Capitan and Half Dome Peak. Rushing water cascades from granite walls above in continuous streams, creating rainbows as it tumbles from Yosemite and Bridalveil Falls.

Mike's dad, William K. Smith, was the town veterinarian. In town, he treated dogs, cats, and other household pets. Out of town, he and his pickup truck, a traveling vet clinic on wheels, also cared for the horses, cattle, sheep, and other livestock of the surrounding ranches. He roamed the entire county, making friends and providing advice and care along the way.

The county appointed Dr. Smith to the official positions of live-stock inspector and pound master, giving him county duties in addition to running his own business. For young Mike, it was so cool to hear Dad on his county radio talking to the dispatcher and the deputy sheriff, and he especially liked listening in on the chatter when he was riding along in the truck. Dad answered to Merced One–Car Fifty-Eight. His own call sign. Even cooler.

Dad had followed his father into the profession. In fact, Mike's grandfather was the first licensed vet in California and had his business a bit to the south in Los Banos, another small and growing valley town. Dad always held out hope that one of his kids might grow up wanting to be a vet too.

Mike had an older brother, Billy, and an older sister, Helen.

Billy, named after his dad, had been injured as a baby. While in the hospital as a newborn, he had been dropped by one of his nurses. His injuries were severe enough to cause polio-like symptoms and some loss of mobility mostly on his left side. In his early years, he underwent several surgeries in attempts to gain additional comfort and function. There was improvement, but Billy was never going to have full function and mobility.

Dad had an intense love of hunting. He loved Billy and took him on his hunting excursions, but Billy was never going to shoulder a rifle the way his dad could, and probably as a result, he never developed much interest in the sport. So as time went on, Billy and his grandpa took up fishing. It was a great way for Billy and Grandpa to be together, and it gave Dad more freedom to hunt on his own.

As Mike grew up, it turned out he was a natural stalker and hunter. Dad now had the beginnings of a hunting partner and relished the opportunity to teach his son some of his shooting skills. Mike learned many marksmanship tricks and techniques from Dad.

Dad worked hard at taking care of the livestock in the county and often needed help with his animal clinic. It was a family business, so for many years, Mike's mom, Winnie Smith, helped in every way she could.

Dad's first clinic and animal hospital was in a military-style Quonset hut on Child's Avenue. Cinder block walls had been erected inside to create workspaces and an office. The walls were seven or eight feet tall but did not reach the domed ceiling, especially in the center of the building. Dad needed Mom's help, and Mike was too young to leave at home. Mom put Mike in one of the cages to play or nap while she assisted with surgery. If he stayed quiet, Mike was allowed to roam. He was curious and wanted to see what they were doing. He was still a little guy, maybe five or six, when he climbed onto the top of the toilet, up onto the toilet tank above, and then up onto the top of the cinder block wall. From there, he scooched on his tummy over to the operating room to peek in from his new perch over their heads.

Over time, Winnie began to react to the ether Doc was using in surgery. She began having respiratory problems from breathing the stuff. One day, Mom came with the news that it was just getting to be too much. She didn't think she could help in the clinic as frequently anymore. Helen, Billy, and Mike were recruited into the position of Dad's new on-call all-around helpers. These were family years.

Dad loved the outdoors, caring for animals, being around ranchers, and, whenever he could, finding time for hunting. Mike remembers being carried out to the duck blinds on cool fall mornings many times before he was even old enough to have his own gun.

Mike got a BB gun at six or seven. Dad let him shoot cans, milk cartons, and empty bottles in the fields out behind the clinic. Very early, he got good at hitting the lizards, birds, dragonflies, and anything else that moved in the dry grass or landed on a tree limb.

A .22 rifle was his at ten. When Mike was twelve, a 20-gauge shotgun was in the long box he had been eyeing under the Christmas tree. Later that Christmas morning, he and Dad were out at the duck blind, waiting. Mike shot his first duck. Not long after, Dad had a rancher friend who doubled as a gunsmith make Mike a 6 mm deer rifle when he was fourteen. At sixteen, Mike was given a brand-new Remington 870 12-gauge pump shotgun by his dad.

Throughout these growing-up years, Mike had one of his guns with him nearly every day. When Mike was a teen, a newly developed cattle vaccine required Dad to travel the county from farm to farm for several weeks to get all the animals treated. There were more than five thousand head of cattle in the county. Dad, Mom, Billy, and Mike lived out of the pickup, seeing rancher after rancher. A twelve-hour day was a short one. Dad liked doing the work and kept at it until dark most days. Mike learned that ranchers work hard and that ranch wives cook well.

Mike was old enough, and Dad's training was good enough that taking guns with them in the pickup to shoot jackrabbits while driving along the levees became one of the best parts of many of the midday trips. They'd spot one, Mike would shoulder the .22 and aim out of the cab window as they drove along. Dad had taught Mike how to lead a moving target and what characteristics each species might have. Jackrabbits have a habit of stopping to look. Mike learned to hold his shot for the stop.

These shots out the window were pointed toward the dirt of the orchard or open field they were crossing. Mike was careful to not shoot when the critters were on a road to avoid possibly bouncing a .22 round into the pasture. Houses were rare in these parts of the county. Dad was clear safety first in all uses of guns.

Dad was patient and offered great tips and advice: "Let your gun track the flight of the bird. Keep pulling your barrel from tail to beak, and as you pass the beak, just keep your barrel moving as you pull the trigger. In this way, the pellets from the discharged shell are sprayed out over a larger span of the flight path, giving you greater likelihood of a hit.

"Doves are quick and fly a level track. Get ahead of them and follow through. Pheasants always rise when they spring; lead them a bit above. Quail are often in coveys on the ground, running in quick spurts, or will sometimes 'jump' and glide in low flight to a nearby clearing." They can be very quick, so Mike got good at leading them with snap shots from the hip.

Mornings or late in the day, when doves were roosting along the levee roads, Dad would let Mike kneel in the bed of the pickup while he leaned up against the bag of grain or the bale of hay for a degree of stability as they drove slowly along. The truck's approach would spring the doves. Mike's shotgun hit easily more than ninety-five out of a hundred.

The family freezer was well stocked. Dad's pride in his son was too.

Mom was a great cook and got very good at preparing whatever her men brought home. One of her tricks was to pack an empty Kentucky Fried Chicken bucket with ten or twelve freshly cleaned dove, fill the pail with water, and freeze it. When the day came to thaw and cook the doves, they were as fresh and new as the day they were taken from the field.

On days Mike was on his own, he would often saddle up his horse, grab the .22, and ride out hunting jackrabbits. It was great fun, and the ranchers liked having less aggravation from the pests. Jackrabbits use their buck teeth to chew and gnaw the bark from the base of nut and fruit trees. Farmers welcomed the help to keep them out of the orchards and away from damaging their crops.

Mom took her kids to church on occasional Sundays. Dad didn't go. Mike remembers wondering why, but Dad didn't talk much about such things. Somewhere he picked up "There is but one God; Mohammed is his name." Dad made this comment frequently, but Mike has no memories of Dad being in any way a religious man. Following Dad's lead, Mike had no active faith either, except when his Mom helped him pray.

Mike was a good bowler and got his first paying job as a pinsetter at the Central Bowl in Merced. He started at twelve and worked there until he left Merced after high school. He did most everything at the alley, including manning the front counter, checking bowlers in, and collecting for the games rolled. A dream at the time was to become a professional bowler. Some nights, the lanes were opened to a men's fifteen-game bowl-a-thon. A prize jackpot, anywhere from fifteen to as much as fifty dollars depending on the number of bowlers in the pool, went to the winner of the most pins toppled. Many nights, Mike knocked down the most or was in the money and went home with fresh bills in his pocket. He had natural hand-eye coordination.

Mike graduated Merced High in '66 and soon after had a freak traffic accident. Mike had taken Dad's pickup down to Fresno to have his new bowling ball drilled. On his way home, a guy towing a trailer changed lanes on Highway 99 in front of Mike. The tarp that was helping secure the load on the trailer flew off and went airborne, flying right onto Mike's windshield. Mike couldn't see a thing ahead. As the trailer slowed in front of him, he slammed into it. This was before seatbelts. On impact, his grip on the steering wheel bent it inward, leaving it with a new set of curves. Dad's truck was totaled.

Mike suffered serious injuries to neck, head, and back. He ended up in the hospital for a spell, then home. Recovery was more than four months. At least for this semester, his next potential lukewarm step toward higher education—enrolling at the local junior college—was out of the question. But honestly, with not much internal drive, Mike's progress toward a college education was fatally stalled.

In fact, Mike was going through a particularly difficult, emotional teenage time. He felt alone and deeply unhappy. Depressed. In his angst and anguish with life, he grabbed and swallowed a bunch of Benadryl out of Dad's lab. He was trying to take a quick exit out of all the stresses and disappointments of his young life.

Winnie had a God nudge come over her. Her internal alarms were sounding. Something was wrong. Suddenly, she knew Mike was in danger; she had to find him, and she went searching. When she found Mike passed out on the lab floor, she screamed, nearly fainting herself, and dashed frantically to call for an ambulance.

Mike remembers being at the hospital and having a view of what was happening in his emergency room from above. It was as if he were somewhere up in a corner of the room. Mom was sobbing in the chair right beside his bed. He saw her. He saw himself lying on the bed. He saw the nurses and doctor dashing about doing this and that to him, seemingly with the greatest concern and skill. He saw a white presence—amazing, glowing white. He felt a sense of peace. He sensed his time might be now.

Then, very subtly, he felt two strong hands firmly gripping his shoulders. It was a feeling of strength that at the same time conveyed a calming softness and gentleness. Like a grandparent's hug, this presence conveyed complete safety, a circle of protection and peace. Like a grandparent, forever perpetual permanent love. Mike felt God say, "I have better things planned for you, my son."

Later, he says about that moment, "God pushed me back into my body. Since that day, the word 'quit,' even the thought of giving up or giving in is no longer a part of my makeup. I'm different now. Quit is no more. I felt a sense of meaning and purpose, even when I had none. I knew at once both that I am loved and that I am needed. I have peace within. I knew He had more for me to do. From then on, I have had God in my life guiding me and protecting me. I know Him. He is with me."

Throughout this time, looking beyond the accident, the lack of academic drive, and even the failed attempt at suicide, his dad could see Mike's potential. He hosted Jack, a good friend and customer, to dinner. Jack was the manager of Miles and Son's Trucking Service in Merced. Miles and Son's was involved in a whole range of projects throughout the state, including a contract to deliver cement powder from the rail line in Marysville to the jobsite of a dam project, Bullard's Bar Dam.

The jobsite in Marysville was quite a bit north of Merced, a good three-hour drive north. Jack was telling Dad he needed a reliable laborer who could follow directions, learn, and take charge of what needed to be done. Dad said, "Mike's available; he can do that." Jack gave Mike the job and helped him get to and from work. He even provided a place for Mike to stay while he was getting started. Mike was eighteen and eager to get going.

Mike is a younger version of his dad. When it's his responsibility, he's all over it. For this job, he was on the road and at the transfer site every morning at six thirty. He was often in the last car out of the lot at night.

A dam project requires many thousand loads of dry cement. Railcars of the dry powder are offloaded into piles at a transfer site. Then from there, the dry powder is augered up from the piles with twelve-inch auger screws onto each truck. For this project, the trucks could make three round trips to and from the dam each day, fourteen or fifteen trucks. Mike and the crew worked fourteen hours a day, every day with a short twelve hours on Sunday. They kept hard at it; in one stretch, they went 111 straight days before having a weekend off. Throughout this first assignment, Mike was always looking for ways to do it faster with less waste and improved efficiency. Soon, he is the go-to guy on locating, staging, and preparing transfer sites.

Jack saw results he liked, and even though Mike was truly just a kid still wet behind the ears, he had the drive and attitude to get the job done. Mike was promoted to construction superintendent. He took pride in his work, learned quickly, and had a get-it-done attitude.

Mike had worked hard enough along this new path that he was earning some real money of his own for the first time in his life. With the many hours he was working at the site, he didn't have much time to go out and spend these earnings. So now, he had some money in his jeans, money left over after his expenses, money in his pocket looking for a good use. It was enough money to go looking for a car. Mike's first car.

His eyes went for a brand spanking new '68 Mustang on the Marysville Ford lot, John C. Bay's Ford. As Mike got to know and became friends with the service manager, Vernon Stoner, they both agreed this was an already cherry car that had some real potential. Vern helped Mike find ways to make his Mustang unique and faster. Mike had seen some of the rich kids in high school take stock cars like his Mustang and turn them into roadsters. Now, it was his turn.

It started out as a gorgeous, eye-catching lime-gold GT 2+2 fast-back. Lime gold, just like it sounds, is that shiny, metal flake version of pea green. Very in and groovy in the day. The coupe came with black leather bucket seats, four on the floor stick shifter, hood locks for style, and a screaming 390 V-8 engine.

Mike added a Detroit Locker 4.10 differential, traction bars, Cyclone headers, an aluminum high-rise intake manifold, and a Holley four-barrel carburetor. The look was finished off with Ansen sixteen-inch polished aluminum racing wheels. As the muscle of his Mustang grew, Mike got better at burying the gas pedal, letting the shifter fly, and burning rubber. That's right, soon he was running the quarter mile in high twelves out at the strip—fast!

Here's an odd thing that happened at the drag strip one night. Bob Denim, a buddy who had a black Mach One 351, came around and said, "Let's race." Bob and Mike mixed it up all the time.

Not far down the road from Marysville is Beale Air Force Base. Beale has some roads, taxi areas, and runways that are not in use— a great place for a late-night drag. Sometimes, the Mustang won; sometimes the Mach One.

Mike in the Mustang and Bob in the Mach One were in a run when a good distance away out on an active runway, the shadow of an Air Force SR-71 Blackbird turned into the wind, set in place for a moment's run-up, and then leaped off the runway and burst like a rocket into the stars and was instantly away.

SR-71s are supersonic spy planes. It had been a glimpse. It was here, and then, streaking through the sky like an arrow, it was gone. It's said that those babies get up and go at over 2,200 mph—crazy fast. Shucks, nearly faster than a speeding bullet.

As that shadow of an aircraft lifted off, both drivers' cars, still in their run sprinting along side by side, instantly lost all electrical— engine, lights, instruments, it all went dark and dead. Both drivers held their lane and coasted down the strip, shaking their heads at each other as they glided to a gradual stop.

They never knew why, but after discussing it a bit, they concluded there must be some new level of unknown magical electronics on that bird.

After the dam contract in Marysville was completed, Miles and Son's and Mike moved on to other projects. Mike's influence and foresight made each new job a bit easier, faster, and more efficient. As they moved from project to project, Mike got to where he could create a transfer station from a bare lot in two days or three at the most. All he needed was a couple of good workers and a backhoe. He had run enough jobs that the layout was in his head. He now knew and could see in his mind how it all needed to be done.

Before long, they shifted to a major improvement of Interstate 8 down in the southern part of California, just north of the border. While working this project, Mike found himself cruising Main Street in El Centro one warm summer evening when he met a young lady out with her girlfriend, both of whom were admiring his Mustang. The cute blonde said, "Nice car. How about giving us a ride?" Mike felt great when girls eyed his car, especially when they complemented it. While they were admiring his Mustang, he was returning the favor, admiring them. Young men and young women have always found creative ways to meet each other. This chance meeting while cruising the strip was a favorite of the day.

Soon, Mike was engaged and off to get married.

Drafted January 3, 1968— Rifle Range Record

Several jobs later, Mike was working on Highway 58 out of Bakersfield in December 1967 when a notice arrived by mail. "Greetings. You will report for an induction physical."

Mike had just turned nineteen on December 1, and now, over a year out of high school, he already had a wife and a daughter. He was in the process of getting his life underway. It was happening. Suddenly, his uncle interrupted it all with this order to report. And he was to report a few days after Christmas.

"Geez, some New Year's present."

Mike had been carrying a 1Y draft card. A 1Y means you have some physical impairment. You can still be called up but only in a time of war.

He rated the 1Y classification due to injuries to his knee that had happened while he was playing Merced High basketball.

Since the war in Vietnam was not a declared war, 1Y was like a free pass from the draft. Yeah, weird logic. Every night on the news, our troops in Vietnam were shown, many times in firefights or just back from some battle. Still, it was not a declared war. They called it the Vietnam "conflict."

Now, with this notice, he was ordered to report for a new physical and potentially could be reclassified. The medical facility he was to report to was clear down in Pomona. That's nearly a three-hour drive south, just east of Los Angeles. And he had to report by 0700. Geez.

After spending that entire day being measured, inspected, probed, and prodded, Mike ended up in front of a rather sloppy US Army sergeant. This soldier's uniform was wrinkled. He was a bit too well nourished around his middle. He conveyed poor bearing and presence. He leaned in with a sneering grin and said, "Well, kid, looks like you are now 1A."

Mike didn't like this guy: "Okay, fine. Will you be mailing me the new card?"

Sgt. with an even bigger sneer: "No, you don't get it. We are going to induct you—today!"

Mike: "Can you do that?"

Sgt. almost getting out of his chair: "I can do anything I f***ing want."

Mike stood there slack faced with another poor slug who just got the same news. A Marine Corps gunnery sergeant appeared out of the next room. This was a big black man, six feet tall and more. His hair was very short, what Mike later learned is high and tight, the way Marines all do their do. His face was ruff, weathered, and confident. His eyes bright and gleaming. He was trim and fit, with a big chest and arms and narrower at the waist. His khaki shirt and dress blue trousers with the long red stripe running down the outer edges was creased, starched, and crisp. His shoes beamed with a sparkling shine. *Wow, this guy is all Marine.*

He asked, "How would you two like to come with me?"

Mike had thought plenty about military service. Heck, Vietnam was all over the news nearly every evening with reports of guys his age fighting in some unpronounceable jungle village somewhere halfway around the world. Guys in his high school class, guys from Merced, were already in.

Just about everyone who had a living room TV growing up had seen war news every night around the dinner table. But Mike was busy. He had things going on. He didn't want to be a soldier, much less a Marine. But this Marine looked sharp.

Suddenly, he was going to be one or the other; a choice had to be made.

Gesturing to the army sergeant, Mike said to the Marine, "Sir, this guy just told me we are going to Fort Ord tonight." Mike had heard on the evening news of a meningitis outbreak at Fort Ord; he didn't want any part of that. Besides, this grumpy army guy with the sloppy uniform had an off-putting, snarky attitude about him. If he could choose, Mike thought, maybe going with this Marine would be better.

"Yeah, he did say that. And what he said is true. But I outrank him," comes back from the gunny.

Mike: "Sir, are you saying I can go with you instead?"

Marine gunny: "That's right, son. You can."

In an act of defiance, Mike gave the army sergeant the bird, his way of waving goodbye, and followed the Marine out of the room, not really knowing much about the difference between the two branches of America's military services.

A few moments later, Mike asked, "Excuse me, Sir, can I call my wife, and, sir, can I call my boss, and, sir, can I let them know I won't be home anytime soon?"

The Marine stopped and turned to Mike, his eyes sparkling. "What did you just call me?"

Mike: "Sir, I said sir."

Chuckling with a big grin, the gunny said, "Sure, you can call them. And, kid, you keep it up, and you are going to do just fine."

Mike made the calls.

First: "I know, baby, it's unbelievable! I'm on my way to the Marines tonight. And, baby, they won't even let me come home. Just this short phone call and one to my boss. Can you believe it? Somehow, you've got to get your sweet tail down here to Pomona, bring the spare key, and get my mustang out of this parking lot. At least get it home. That way you can use it while I'm away. Will you go to your parents? I'm sorry, baby. I miss you already. I'll call you as soon as I can. Probably in a couple of weeks. Until then, love you. Bye."

Second: "Yeah, I can't believe it. They drafted me just like that. I'm going to be in San Diego at the Marine Corps Recruit Depot tonight. Can you believe it? They've got a bunch of us getting on the bus in a few minutes. I don't know when I'll be able to come back to work. I think it's for a couple of years. Could you mail my last check? That way my wife will be able to deposit it. I'll give you a call when I can. Bye."

Marine Corps Recruit Depot (MCRD) is everything Marine boot camp has always been. Golden footsteps painted on the pavement for the scrambling recruits to occupy as they come spilling out of the bus to a chorus of screaming drill instructors. New labels: Maggot. Children. Ladies.

Mike learned fast. Shut up, pay attention, do what you are told, and scream, "Sir, yes, sir!" But only when you are specifically addressed.

Buzz haircuts. Box up and mail your civvies home. You won't need them. Here's how you make a rack. Do it. Run everywhere, start before dawn, quit with the formal instruction and continuous harassment just a bit before lights out. Use any excess time to square yourself and your area away.

Unit runs, unit classes, unit PT, unit meals, unit drills. Everyone in the platoon shares the same Quonset hut, the same showers, and the same latrine. Yes, you will have a turn cleaning it. No, not much personal privacy. That's ok. You are running in and out while being encouraged along by a squared-away Marine with a very loud voice. No time for privacy.

Drill instructors are selected for their bearing and attention to all things Marine. To recruits, they often start as harassers and morph over time into kindly brothers, uncles, and sometimes father figures. And some of them no one ever likes.

History. The founding of the Corps. Tun Tavern. Captain Sam Nichols. Battles fought, wars won, heroes of the Corps. John Basilone. Chesty Puller. Carlos Hathcock. Every Marine a rifleman, every resource in support of the rifleman. War stories, films, great quotes: "Retreating? Like hell! We're just attacking in another direction." And every time anything happens that pleases a drill instructor, "Hoorah! Everyone shouts at the top of their lungs back, "Hoorah!" Marines love "Hoorah!"

John Basilone was a hero of World War II. Chesty Puller a hero of the Korean War and a leader that was famous for looking out for his men, saving peoples behinds in many tough fights. A Marine's Marine.

Carlos Hathcock was a Vietnam war scout/sniper with over ninety confirmed kills. The North Vietnamese had put a $50,000 bounty on Hathcock. His most famous shot was directly through the scope of his assassin's rifle. In telling that story, he often said, "I got lucky, pulling my trigger first. My squeeze beat his by a hair."

Throughout it all, the recruits were treated as equals. Work hard, listen, practice, drill, get better.

"You are a part of America's finest fighting force. Your training will prepare you for battle. It will be tough enough that you will feel ready when you get to combat."

Instructors and recruits alike knew that most of them would be in Vietnam soon.

Night low crawls with live ammo, a tracer every fifth round. Spraying .50 caliber from one position, .30 caliber from another. Live ammo. Eighteen to twenty-four inches off the deck.

There was no confusion about purpose.

Mike had a physically demanding job before MCRD, providing him with a significant fitness advantage over many other recruits who struggled to keep up with the runs and PT. He entered boot camp at buff 165 pounds and graduated thirteen weeks later at a firmer, more muscled 165 pounds. This same weight at the ending was an anomaly among graduates. Most recruits that came in flabby ending up losing over ten pounds with all the physical training, running, and drills. Mike firmed and pumped up. It showed.

His performance, attention to detail, and clear drive brought Mike and a couple others in his platoon an early promotion to Pfc.—Private First Class, E-2.

Mike's drill instructor, Staff Sgt. Henry, taught honor, respect, discipline, and love of God and country: "God created the Marine Corps to protect America so that Americans could worship God." This guy was so good, everyone admired him. Mike wanted to be more like him.

Here's an event that helped Mike earn his early promotion. Along the progression in boot camp, Mike had a stint on kitchen patrol (KP) just like everyone else. It was near the end of the week; an inspection was coming.

The mess hall sergeant barked, "You people better have it ready."

Mike was assigned the freezers and refrigerators. Everything had to be pulled off the shelves; then they were scrubbed and wiped down, top to bottom, and everything was put back. It had to be immaculate. Mike made it so.

Later that afternoon, Mike spotted a noncommissioned officer (NCO) of another platoon, a sergeant, strolling through the kitchen. Mike noticed that this guy spent quite a bit of time alone in the refers. After he was gone, Mike did a full walk-through, checking for anything out of place. He discovered several frozen food items were now on top of a freezer. *Well, look at that. Maybe that sergeant was trying to ensure his guys and his platoon finished ahead of us in this week's inspection.*

Mike removed the items, got them back to the freezer where they belonged, and cleaned the entire area. Once again, it was spotless, immaculate.

For the first time in anyone's memory, the mess area and freezers passed inspection. For his diligence, persistence, and attention to details, S/Sgt. Henry recommended Mike for meritorious promotion to Pfc. The inspection helped. It was his consistent drive, perseverance, and enthusiasm that made the difference and earned him the rank.

Toward the end of boot camp, two weeks of intensive rifle training began. The first week was day after day of dry firing (no live ammunition). All Marines learn to create a firm aiming posture in four positions: standing, sitting, kneeling, and prone. Orientation, instruction, and practice are provided on sight picture, frame, use of the sling for greater stability, trigger pull, breath control, distance, and wind adjustments. For the entire first week, recruits practiced snapping in and taking aim with no ammo.

Each recruit was given a marksmanship and data book. This loose-leaf notebook had training tips and illustrations of appropriate sight picture, trigger control, wind effect, zeroing, and so on. Further in, the notebook had scoring pages for recording of all the facts on each round sent to the target when the shooting began.

Here's a couple of paragraphs from the notebook on trigger control:

"Trigger control is a vital element in producing an accurate shot. The trigger action must be accomplished so as not to disturb the position of the rifle when the shooter has his sights aligned. The results of a good steady position, perfect sight alignment, proper aiming point, and accurate correction for wind are of no value unless precise trigger control is achieved.

"The primary consideration in trigger control is that the trigger be moved straight back toward the rear smoothly, gradually, and evenly—that is, sque-e-e-ezed. Any pressure, however slight, to the side, up or down, that is applied to the trigger during this rearward movement will be transmitted to the rifle, and a wide, high, or low shot will likely result."

Range masters and shooting instructors were beside every shooter, nearly one-on-one. Many recruits had never seen or even held a rifle before. Every Marine had to become proficient at using his weapon. Live fire needed to be safe. Recruits found that the range instructors had great tips and advice. It was just difficult for them to settle down and get their personal aiming technique to match all the details of the instruction.

On qualification day, each shooter fired fifty rounds. First was thirty rounds slow fire at bull's-eye targets. The bull's-eye was ten inches across at one and three hundred yards, twenty inches at five hundred. Shooters were allowed up to sixty seconds per round. From two hundred yards, ten rounds were fired offhand and standing. When completed and it was all clear on the firing line, shooters moved back one hundred yards to fire five rounds sitting then five rounds kneeling at three hundred yards. They moved back once more to fire their final ten rounds while prone from the five-hundred-yard line.

The next twenty rounds were scored shooting rapid fire. Here shooters fired ten shots in bursts within ten seconds. It was not automatic fire. It was ten trigger pulls in under ten seconds. That's why trigger control was so important. Newer shooters tend to pull down in rapid fire.

S/Sgt. Henry came over to Mike after watching him fire and be scored on prequal day. There were many white scoring disks going up centered on his target indicating the last round was in the bull's-eye. "Hey, Smith, you're shooting pretty well. Who taught you?"

Mike: "Sir, my dad, sir!"

S/Sgt. Henry: "Well, hoorah mister, it looks like he taught you well. Tomorrow, I'm putting you on the far left on the range where I can watch how you do. Shoot for qualification the way your dad taught. I have a feeling you can do very, very well. I will take care of Sergeant Lindsay too. I'll make sure he's somewhere else, so he doesn't mess with you."

Lindsay was one of the drill instructors that no one liked. He was a short man. People said he had a Napoleon complex. He had his favorites to seek out and harass each day. He relished giving recruits a new daily ration of his wisdom and colorful vocabulary. He delighted in getting into their faces. Mike was one of his favorites in this cycle. Almost every recruit knows someone like Lindsay.

On qualification day, Mike was on. He fired a range record of 248 out of a possible 250. His ten rapid-fire rounds while prone at five hundred yards were perfect, all fives. No recruit had shot 248 before. No boot had been perfect at five hundred yards.

Mike did have two rounds score fours at three hundred yards while kneeling. Those were the two rounds out of fifty he had outside the five ring of the bull's-eye. He gave credit and blame to his bum knee.

To earn the Marine Corps rifle expert badge, shooters must achieve 220 or better. Mike had wanted to earn it, and now he rated that badge by an impressive margin. He'd be wearing the crossed rifles at graduation.

Later that afternoon, with his platoon back in the Quonset hut preparing for chow, Mike and another recruit got called out to go see the lieutenant, the platoon commander. *Oh no, now what?* His mind started racing. *What could it be?* Recruits don't ever get called to see the lieutenant unless it's trouble.

The lieutenant took them to the captain's office, the company commander. *Holy Moses, the company commander?*

As they marched into the room and popped to attention, the mouthwatering aroma of the two Big Macs and an order of large fries wafted from the familiar white McDonald's bags sitting next to the tall ice-filled cups of Coke.

The lieutenant announced, "Gentlemen, that was some fine shooting today. We thought you'd like a bit of a treat."

The other recruit had shot 238, well over the 220 minimum for expert, and in many cycles, his would have been the best score of the day.

The captain turned to Mike and said, "No other boot has shot what you did today—248. And no boot has been perfect at five hundred yards. You were 100 percent. Congratulations, Marine. That was some fine shooting today. You have done so well that we're recommending both of you for scout/sniper school. It's where our best shooters train to be outstanding. It's an elite shooters school. It will prepare you to use your impressive shooting skills to protect other Marines.

In addition, to be eligible to attend this school, you must be a lance corporal, E-3, so you will pick up that promotion at the school as well. When you graduate that school, you'll rate another promotion to corporal. The school is at Camp Lejeune, North Carolina. One of our instructors there is Gunnery Sergeant Carlos Hathcock. Yes, that Carlos Hathcock."

Both recruits were handed the bags and drinks as they were dismissed back to S/Sgt. Henrys' hooch to inhale their rewards. Recruits are always hungry.

When the end of boot camp arrived and his platoon filed past the dignitaries and guests, Mike was surprised and excited to find his parents' faces in the stands for his graduation. They made the over eight-hour trip down from Merced and now were watching from the stands with the battalion dignitaries, the wives, girlfriends, moms, dads, and other assorted family as the graduates marched in review. They listened with admiration and pride as the commanders congratulated the new Marines on their progress and success. It was a big day.

The Marine band marching with the troops played "The Star-Spangled Banner." The spiffed up, squared-away Marines moved in precision formations as each parent's glistening eyes searched for his platoon, his face. These new Marines had drilled and drilled to prepare for this day. They moved sharply in unison, each heel striking the deck together, each movement happening throughout the formations as one. The band played the stirring "Marine's Hymn," bringing chills up the spines of all present. "From the halls of Montezuma…" Hearts swelled with pride.

When it is over and you are standing with your son, he is looking his fittest ever. His posture, uniform, and bearing are all Marine. They have cleaned him up, made him conform, and changed him forever. He is proud, handsome, and happy. He looks so grown up in that uniform.

"I love a man in uniform."

He has become more confident, more mature, and more alive. The Marines have changed him. For many, it's a change they never outlive.

Still, in the back of your mind, there is the constant unspoken reality of his being one step closer to war. He has been training to be a Marine. Most of these new Marines will be going to Vietnam. Most Marines are grunts. Grunts carry rifles out in the jungle, looking to go to battle. Grunts shoot at our enemies. Grunts get shot at. Some get wounded, some die. Everyone knows. It's a day of pride, a day of patting him on the back, and a day of deep underlying fear and, for some, personal moments of private tears. This graduation day, maybe even for Mike's mom and dad.

Scout/sniper school is on the East Coast, Camp Lejeune, North Carolina. They were trained with Springfield M1A1 Super Match M14 rifles. Nine-times scope, chromed stainless steel twenty-four-inch barrel, four lug bolt. Mike learned more about concealment, target identification, shot selection, assignment protocol, and insertion/extraction.

Marine commanders use scout/snipers to gather direct intelligence of enemy activity in the field and to selectively kill key enemy leaders in direct defense of US and Allied forces.

Gunnery Sergeant Hathcock, or Carlos as he preferred to be addressed by his students, was a soft-spoken redneck hillbilly from the Ozarks. He learned his outdoors skills as a kid out in the hills hunting with his dad, just like Mike had. Carlos relished training his students, fellow Marines, on survival tips and techniques. He told stories, sharing his experiences and the methods he used to kill and survive during his years of success in the field. He told his students that if they would operate the way he instructed them, they would survive, too. If they did not, good luck. Confirmed kills require either a direct witness or the recovery of a body part. Many of Carlos's missions were alone. Many of his targets were too far away to risk trying to retrieve evidence of the strike. Carlos had ninety-three confirmed with his probable kills being closer to three hundred. He was a master at it.

Besides the shot through the scope of a North Vietnamese sniper, Carlos is famous for many other difficult missions. In one stretch of several days, he laid waiting silently in an open field for the right moment to take his shot at a particular general. He was ready when his prey stepped out in his morning answer to natures call.

Mike saw Carlos shoot. He was impressive. Here's a guy that was that much better. Mike honed his shooting skills and learned to become silent, invisible, and undetectable.

PRELUDE TO BONUS CONVERSATIONS

Wow, an amazing story, right? Ahead, you'll find bonus segments of conversations Mike and I had along the way as we worked together to gather more details, topics, and specifics. Included are some of his best stories. The titles of each conversation may help you decide if you have enough interest to read on. We used the transcribing app Otter AI to take notes of our conversations. Much of what we spoke about follows verbatim. After our first conversation, I knew the basics of what had happened. Mike and I sat together over several weeks talking in each of these conversations, exploring what came to mind, working on filling in the details. What emerged expands on the story and lets us hear more about him, his life, how he trained, and what it was like living at war in Vietnam. Each conversation brings out more explanation, more color, and more understanding. Some material will feel a bit redundant, in that much of what he brought out in these conversations is now in the story of the final mission. When you hear it again, details help clarify and provide us with greater understanding. Some of the conversations are Mike telling interesting side stories. I found myself trying to fill in what had happened and how it had affected Mike. I wondered many times how I would have done in his place. Or in the place of any of his fellow Marines serving as grunts. As Mike talks, we learn more about him and how he adapted and coped as well as gain new insights and new perspectives. The sequence of the chapters follows the sequence of our conversations.

"The Final Conversation" and the "Thanks and Appreciation" chapters you read earlier happened after all the detail gathering of the bonus conversations and as you have seen are meant to close out his story. When you have finished reading the bonus conversations, you may find you want to come back and reread "The Final Conversation" and "Thanks and Appreciation". I found after hearing it all, I wanted to say thank you again.

There are very few Marines with Mike's level of marksmanship. Very few who are asked to use these unique skills to do what he was doing. Stalking, targeting and killing individual enemy leaders. How do you live with what you have seen, what you have done?

After hearing Mike tell about all that he had done trying to save Jonathan, his enormous physical effort, and then listening to Mike talk of the even greater ache in his heart over his feelings of loss and grief, our conversations continued digging into that part of the story to give Mike a chance to vent it all out.

You may notice that as the conversations go on, the details get more intense, telling us more of what our Marines experienced.

WHO WROTE YOU UP?—
RIFLE INSPECTION

Phil: "What did you take out in the field to eat on your assignments?"
Mike: "Most of the time, nothing. Many assignments were out and back within a day, so we took nothing to eat or, if anything, Hershey bars. Hershey made special bars just for the military. These bars were less prone to softening in the heat than the ones at a grocery store. They'd last a couple of days in our bags. Sadly, they were nowhere near as sweet either. They would give us quick energy to keep us going. You were still hungry, but you felt like you had enough in your tank to keep going.

"Besides, we had adrenaline out in the bush. We were naturally on super high alert. We liked the Hershey bars, too, because they were small, and all we needed to carry out was the wrapper. We left nothing behind from our missions. Anything we took in, we took out. We even tried to take out our brass, the shell casings of expended rounds. We didn't want the NVA soldiers that were trying to find and kill us to have any advantage or to be aware of where we had been. Scout/snipers come and go undetected, or we don't survive.

"C rations were coming into use during this time, but we didn't like carrying them. They tend to be too bulky and too much weight. We preferred carrying extra bullets to carrying food. I always liked having extra rounds. It gave me a warm feeling. Remember, we were out there alone. Sometimes, just me and what I carried, sometimes just us two. Besides, the C rats cartons and cans are a nuisance to carry out, too bulky, too much potential to make noise. Leave the food, take the bullets.

"I became a Christian during that time but just not in public. I'm quite sure He looked over me. Because of the things I did. I was dropped off in the jungle, or I hiked in. That put me out in the field with the enemy two-thirds of my time. I had no radio. No way to call for help. Sometimes I was on an assignment with a specific target, sometimes out collecting information on who was out there. I would try to see and report back what they were doing. Sometimes alone, sometimes with a spotter. Not always Jonathan. I had many opportunities to be alone when I was out there and have a talk with God. We got well acquainted. I'm a loner. Most snipers are. It was good to have that relationship.

"When I was hit by that grenade, most people would have given themselves a shot of morphine for the pain of the wounds I had inflicted. But I didn't feel I needed it with all the adrenaline pumping through me. Adrenaline is probably the strongest drug in the whole wide world that people don't understand. I never felt hardly any—well, I did have pain, but not unbearable pain, until I saw that chopper coming down to pick us up. Then it really hurt.

"God was with me then, and that has everything to do with me making it back. There's no question in my mind. He was good to me. He has been good to me since."

Phil: "Who do you think wrote you up for the Bronze Star?"

Mike: "Most likely it was the navy corpsman. The guy that worked on me. It must have been him or one of the crew on the helicopter that came in to get us. He could have done the write-up sometime after I was already back at Balboa Naval Hospital in San Diego.

"We had been on several prior missions with transport in and out on Hueys. It's possible it was someone else on Katye's crew. Those extraction crews flew out of many other battles with KIA and WIA Marines, but this time, we were a bloody mess crawling when they came for us.

"On each of our prior missions, two of us would get aboard their Huey with scout/sniper gear—grease paint, weapons, sidearms, ammo, and determination. We were carrying scout/sniper rifles with scopes. Grunts had M16s. We went out alone or in pairs. We were a bit different and stood out as different. The aircrews knew what we were about. They were briefed. They knew enough of our assignment to know where to take us and where to come to get us. After each prior mission, we had always been at the extraction point at the earliest pickup time. Never late, always there. And of course, this time when they came down on this final run to get us, I had collapsed under Jonathan. He was wrapped to me. I couldn't move him off me. I couldn't move at all. I was done.

"It is hard, though, to know who did the write-up. It had to be a witness, someone who was there, and most likely that person thought about it for some time. I think that's why it took forever before I even knew about it. It had to be one of the four that came to get us: two pilots, the crew chief, and the corpsman. It could have been submitted even after I was already discharged five months later in June 1970. It must have been that when the citation was ultimately approved that I was already discharged. If they sent out a notice to my address of record, I never got it.

"I think it was the corpsman because he was trying to keep me—number one—awake. He saw that I had lost a good bit of blood. He talked to me to see how awake I was. I don't know what I looked like when he got to us but I'm guessing not too good. Number two, he wanted me not focusing on my knee and Jonathan's death. He saw my grief, my anguish, how the pain of it affected me. Maybe what he saw, he told someone. Maybe that person suggested to him to write it up. That entire crew could have decided who would write it up."

Phil: "So Jonathan was gone when the corpsman got to you?"

Mike: "Yeah, he was gone. Probably he died an hour or so before we got picked up, I just didn't realize it. I was checking him about every hour. The last time was a bit more than an hour before. I just couldn't believe it."

Phil: "Initially, was he able to talk to you?"

Mike: "He was at first, but then with his pain, he had to have the morphine. He passed out after the second one. He pretty much was asleep. Which is what I wanted; you know. The pain he was in was intense, more than too much. He had to have the morphine. The way I knew he was alive was with his pulse and his breathing.

"I spoke to him several times as we crawled—I mean, I crawled—trying to keep him going. 'Hang in there, Marine.' Several times on the way. Things like that. Hoorah! I was hoping to encourage him, keep him going."

Phil: "He bled out?"

Mike: "Yeah, internally, yeah. He probably passed, and I just didn't know it. He was limp anyway. It wasn't one of those moments like you see in the movies or on TV where I would have had him in my lap and all that stuff. I didn't even know he was gone until the corpsman turned from Jonathan back to me. I couldn't believe it."

Phil: "It had to break your heart."

Mike: "Oh, it did. For sure. Every day, still does."

Phil: "The flight out and insertion for this mission happened near midnight, right?"

Mike: "Yeah, we knew it would take us three to four hours in the dark to get from the drop-off point to the place I had in mind to set up our hide."

Phil: "No lights? How did the pilots get into the LZ?"

Mike: "Yeah, no lights. All the external lights—off. Even the lights on the top of the airframe and the rotor blade tip lights were off. No position lights. Just on the instrument panels, the red night vision lights were on. They glowed a soft red. Red light doesn't negatively affect night vision. These pilots, they were good. They had been to this LZ before, so they had scoped it out."

Phil: "Yeah, but to land in the dark, the pilots are using the barometric altimeter and the radar altimeter gauges on their instrument panel along with their external scan of what terrain they can see to judge elevation off the deck. Then they're searching, trying to get a decent visual on the ground in the glow of the moonlight, to set up for the landing or hover. It's not difficult flying lickety-split at night when you are working off of instruments over the valley on the way to the LZ. You are at a high enough altitude that there are no worries. But to hover on instruments in the dark is just not possible. You need to see the deck. To hover in nearly complete darkness in moonlight will make even good sticks shiver. It's just not easy to get a good scan going. It's an advantage that they flew only red lights out. At least their night vision is in full effect."

Mike: "Like I said, these guys were good. As they dropped us off, they never even touched down. They came in, slipping down into a low hover, I mean just a few feet over the LZ, and then they tapped us to jump out. They were only there for a moment.

"Those guys flew so much; they had the feel for it."

Phil: "Yeah, I know. I got to the place where I crawled into the cockpit and strapped in, putting the aircraft on. It was a part of me. When I moved, it moved with me.

"Huey pilots sit adjacent to each other up in the bubble-like cockpit with the windscreens and nose glass giving them unrestricted visibility and vulnerability. The side doors had been removed to make room for the mounting of an M60 machine gun and to make it easier for troops to jump out or back on. There's room behind the pilots in the cabin for the crew chief plus four or five passengers.

"The M60 machine gun slung in the door is belt fed with canisters of ammo below. That gun fires about six hundred rounds a minute. The crew chief standing in the door operating the gun is the crews' protection with the corpsman as backup. The crew chief plugs his flight helmet in to the comm system, which lets him take instruction and pass information to the pilots. They would have flown over this terrain before and would be using navigation aids on their instrument panel to help them confirm the LZ's location. Hueys have TACAN, VOR, and ADF needles built in the RMI. The RMI—Radio Magnetic Indicator—is their compass.

"Back at the squadron, the inserting crew would have logged the drop-off location with the operations desk so the pickup crews could use it later when they go out looking for them. They would have noted visual reference points as well, things like how far from a trail, how close to a river, where on the rice paddy. They are trying to help out their buddies. There are only so many crews supporting Marines. These are guys that live, eat, drink, and sometimes die together. They work very hard to keep the last from happening."

Mike: "The crews looking for us at the extraction times knew where to start looking. We may have crawled to where we weren't expected or supposed to be.

"I never got the corpsman's name. It's sad to have missed that chance; he was very good with my leg and knee. I do think one of the pilots was Rusty. There were the two pilots, the crew chief, and the corpsman. Three Marines and the navy corpsman on the Huey when Jonathan and I went in and when they came to take us out.

"It must have been the crew chief that was helping with me and Jonathan when they came running because there were two working on us. The pilots never shut down or got out of the Huey. They were uncomfortable sitting there and anxious to get out of that LZ. They didn't like being on the deck, sitting in that cockpit, turbines and rotors turning, waiting for us to get scraped up while they had to just sit 'stationary' like a sitting duck in 'no-man's land.'

"They put Jonathan on the floor. And all of our gear, weapons, ammo, and such. They set me up and belted me in to one of the web seats so the corpsman could work on my leg. He started an IV because I had lost a lot of blood."

Phil: "Were you conscious all the way back?"

Mike: "I was. In fact, I was in more pain on the way back than I was on the whole ordeal of crawling out. He gave me a pretty good shot of morphine, and they took me right into an operating room when we landed."

Phil: "There was a medical crew to take you off Katye?"

Mike: "Yeah, they had radioed ahead that a surgeon was needed ASAP. They landed at the medivac hotspot. So right into a field OR [operating room] where they worked on my leg for a couple of hours and did all they could. When I came to and could talk, they said they thought the leg could be saved. So, I was on a plane out of there, like right now. They took me straight from Vietnam to the Naval Hospital in San Diego, Balboa. And there they had an orthopedist and right into surgery again. I was told later that they had a lot of scraping to do on the bones and some cartilage to repair, plus shrapnel to remove. They put it all back together. I was on crutches for, gosh, a month. I had feeling in my foot; they were happy about that. After about two more months, I was released back to Camp Pendleton."

Phil: "What did you do while you were recuperating?"

Mike: "We were doing physical therapy every day. I got to where I could jog a little bit and everything, and that's when they released me back to active duty."

Phil: "How long was this from when you were drafted?"

Mike: "It was June 8, 1970. That's the date of separation on my DD 214, June 8, 1970. I was twenty-one. I was drafted January 3, 1968, at nineteen. Just a month shy of two and a half years total Marine Corps time.

"My dad had graduated veterinarian medical school from Texas A&M and served as a captain until the end of WWII. A&M had a policy of free tuition to offspring of graduates. But young and stupid, I found I liked electronics more, and then with my accident in his truck, I never made it to A&M."

Phil: "Texas A&M is known for having a very strong ethos. Would you say that shaped your dad's character?"

Mike: "I would say my grandfather shaped my father's character. My grandfather was a very strict, stern person. My father was a very strict, stern person. He definitely shaped, between him and the Marine Corps, shaped my personality. He had high expectations for the people around him. But he'd never belittle anybody. Okay, he was the type of person—he worked the crap out of you. But he would reward you for your efforts.

"Both my Dad and Granddad were guys that never showed much emotion. I tend to take after them. When my grandfather was killed in a car wreck, it was like, okay, we have this stuff we've got to take care of. I didn't see any remorse in his face. The only time I saw my father cry was when one of our hunting dogs, his favorite, a black lab, was killed. He cried over Sheba. I did too. She had followed my car when I left for high school and had been hit on the highway. When I got home and came looking for her, he couldn't tell me what had happened. He tried. It turned out that she had followed my car that morning as I headed out and evidently had still been chasing after me when she was hit. He had gone looking for her when she didn't come back home, found her dead, and had taken her and put her body in his hospital so we could bury her later. Then he had kept an eye out for me to come tell me what had happened when I got home. He knew Sheba and I were tight. When I was home, she was beside me tail wagging so hard she couldn't stand still. I loved that dog. He loved her, I won't say more, but probably just as much. He starts telling me what had happened, and we both broke down. We both stood there and sobbed and sobbed. Tears everywhere. Finally, he turned and went back to work. That was a terrible, terrible day, but I never felt closer to my Dad."

Phil: "Your dad seemed to have a troubled life to a degree, or was it just the way he was raised?"

Mike: "I'd say just the way he was raised. My grandfather was the same way. I'm just now learning how to show emotions."

Phil: "Was he a Christian?"

Mike: "No, that was the one downside. Later, Dad had open-heart surgery. He was a heavy drinker, heavy smoker, borderline alcoholic. Always up at 5:00 a.m. Always at the job. Never failed."

Phil: "What was his beverage of preference?"

Mike: "I never saw him with a beer. It was either whiskey or gin. Chapman and Gore, I think was the brand of whiskey. I don't even think they make it anymore.

"I remember his first hospital being in a Quonset hut. It had cinder block walls and partitions and cages for the dogs or other animals. My mom helped my dad when he operated. I wanted to watch. That's when I got creative and climbed on top of the wall. At first, watching what he was doing was gross. It was bloody. Still, I wanted to watch. I was impressed. Dad was a skilled surgeon.

"I didn't realize they were using ether to put the animals under. I developed a tolerance to ether. Now, I love the smell of ether. When they went to take my tonsils out, they couldn't put me under because they were trying to use ether. My dad got a big kick out of that. They had to give me sodium pentothal, which was still in its infancy.

"The state transportation people came in one day, gave him a check, and said you have one year to move. They were putting a new freeway in, probably I-5, and it was going right through the middle of this, so eminent domain or whatever. They gave him a fair price. He turned around and bought five acres of land out on Highway 140. Built a new hospital, and we built a new home right behind the hospital.

"I can remember even very young, six or seven, going out with my mom and dad to the duck blinds. My dad, on a lot of those mornings, would be carrying me out on his shoulders. I liked being up that high. One of my kid memories is spotting a log or something floating down the stream where we were. Whatever it really was, I thought for sure I was seeing an alligator. I was scared silly but kept my mouth shut.

"Dad was probably the best shot I've ever seen in my life. He hunted duck, pheasant, quail, deer, bear, and wild boar. We were out together many, many times.

"My dad was most of the ranchers' personal doctor, too. Yes, he was a vet and cared for their livestock, but for some of them, they also used him as their own personal doc. They knew him, trusted him and many times found if they told him what was going on he would offer then excellent people healing advice. One quick story—a rancher named Horace Meyers, no upper-level education. I mean just eighth grade. He ends up a multimillionaire rancher of thousands of acres up in the foothills. He and my dad, they were very close friends. One night, Horace showed up at our house. I answered the front door.

"He says, 'Your dad here?' I brought him in.

"He says, 'Doc, I think I have anthrax.'

"Dad says, 'Well, we're going to take you to the hospital then.'

"He says, 'Nope. No hospital. You're taking care of me.'

"So, I lost my bed for ten days. And my dad doctors Horace Meyers back to health. That's how much respect he had in the ranching community. They all loved my dad.

"Have you ever heard of the brucellosis epidemic? It was a communicable disease back in the '50s. The federal government mandated that every cow, every head of cattle, sheep, or whatever livestock be vaccinated. So every weekend for two years, we'd pack up our stuff and hit one, two, three ranches a day. Sometimes vaccinate up to five, six hundred head of cattle a day. I think he was paid thirty or fifty cents a head to vax and mark the cattle. They had metal fold-over ear tags that went on with a pliers and a tag that got slapped on their back.

"We'd get up three, four in the morning and head to the first ranch. Each ranch tried to get all their cattle in, often moving them to us from more than one field. They were doing their best to get every critter done so they didn't need to have us come back. Yeah, so we'd work until noon.

"The ranchers' wives would show up about noon time bringing out a lunch spread that would put even professional cooks to shame. I mean steak, beans, corn bread, you know. So much wonderful food. No alcohol but tea, water. We had our lunch break with just a few minutes of conversation or potty break, then we'd start at it again and vaccinate until dusk. Those ranch people were very kind, friendly, and neighborly. Hard working, solid people mostly."

Phil: "How old were you?"

Mike: "Eight, nine, about in there. I was pretty young. I was old enough to get in on the ear tagging part of the process. My hand almost fit the pliers.

"Dad did livestock pregnancy tests. All the ranchers got to know him. They gave him keys to their gates to make it easier for him to provide the care they needed. And you know there were several good-size ranches in the county. We were driving to them all the time. We would go out, and during dove season, we'd be driving along a levee road early in the day or more toward the end of the day, and the truck's movement along the levee would jump the dove. There'd be a bale of hay and a sack of grain in the back of the pickup. I'd ride back there, leaning up against the hay or grain, sometimes with my knee down on the floor for stability and pop the doves with my shotgun. He'd be driving slowly—five, seven miles an hour. And I would shoot the flying dove out of the moving pickup as we went."

Phil: "I'm guessing you tried to pop them all?"

Mike: "Yeah, and they are going every direction. I'd shoot and reload, roll a bit further, shoot and reload. I was good for ninety-five out of one hundred. Each time we went out, I'd have shotgun shells in my vest ready to go. You know, the Lord gifted me with the ability to shoot. Dad had a great time watching and coaching my shooting as we went.

"I qualified about three weeks ago for my open-carry permit."

Phil: "With a pistol?"

Mike: "Yeah. Semiautomatic."

Phil: "How far?"

Mike: "Three to fifteen yards. Fifty rounds."

Phil (looking at the holes in Mike's target): "You have a perfect score."

Mike: "I have never not fired a perfect score."

Phil: "How many guns do you have?"

Mike: "A lot."

Phil: "I know, but is that ten, twelve? You don't know for sure? Okay, how many long guns?

Mike: "I have two. At one time, I owned the same rifle as Carlos and I used, a civilian version. It's the same, just not automatic. I sold it. We called it White Feather in his honor. It's what he was known as when he was hunting in the field. Sort of his call sign. He had a white feather on the end of his barrel out in the jungle of Vietnam. I needed the money for something else. It was maybe twenty years ago. I got $3,600. The technical name is the Springfield M1A1 National Match M14."

Phil: "And this is the same weapon you were carrying on the final mission?"

Mike: "Yes, that's what we both were carrying. In Vietnam, the job designation would determine what I carried."

Phil: "But on that particular mission, you carried the M1A1, and you carried a sidearm?"

Mike: "Yeah, .45 caliber pistol."

Phil: "K bar knife?"

Mike: "Oh yes, I still have the K bar under my bed at night. I just feel better having it and a few guns around.

"My first, my son Chris, was conceived on the first base liberty when I was at Camp Pendleton at Infantry Training Regiment after boot camp. We were told if the whole company passes rifle inspection, we'd get a weekend pass. I found out from other guys that nobody had ever passed. Marines can be tough when it comes to inspections.

"A company is three or more platoons. A platoon is three or more squads, usually fifty Marines in a platoon. Nearly two hundred of us all together.

"Turns out the night before inspection, they had scheduled us for night maneuvers. We knew we'd be using tracer rounds with every fifth round looking like an orange streak leaving its visual trail in the night sky. It's like streaming fireworks with bullets. Machine guns are like hoses. You know, night maneuvers.

"Well, cleaning out the barrel after it's been shooting tracers, it's no fun. Tracers leave lots of residue. So I'm a squad leader, there's four of us. We four are first at the range. We shoot our weapons and just passed them down the line to the next four. We leave our weapons, and the next platoon, then heck the whole company, shoots with just those four rifles. We get in, and the M16, you can just take that one in the shower with you. By the way, that's just a saying. No one actually showers with it.

"But the point of that statement is that the M16 is easy to clean. We had all learned how to clean our rifles with many nights of preparing for just this kind of inspection. This night, everyone has a turn concentrating on cleaning, but now we just have the four rifles that have been fired. After being cleaned once, each fired rifle is worked on by three or four other Marines. I mean cleaning rods through the barrels, toothbrushes cleaning every joint and crease, Q-tips poking the crevices, finished with a very light coat of oil. Then wiped dry with a soft cloth, leaving the barrel with a spotless gleam. Finally, any speck of dust or lint was brushed off with a small paintbrush. These weapons are clean. Sparkling clean. We had been working at making things clean for a while, we had learned well and knew what we were doing. Every Marine that had an unfired clean weapon passes his already clean, unfired rifle to his bunkmate for one final pre-inspection inspection and wipe down. Clean making clean.

"We're setting up the next morning, it's Friday morning, for the inspection. Two hundred rifles. We've got a couple ponchos laid out there on the grinder with all two hundred of them lined up in rows. The sergeant, he picks up the first weapon. That was mine. He gives it a healthy dose of eyeballing. It's spotless. So are all my buddies'. He tromps back into the barracks, comes stomping back out with a roll of toilet paper and a pair of white gloves. He was pissed.

"He went back to picking them up and inspecting, trying. But he couldn't find a speck on anybody's weapon. So finally, he found out what had happened. He calls us four into his little office. He says, 'You guys think you're pretty fricken' smart, don't ya? Now, I've got to be the first damn platoon leader to give a base liberty. What were you thinking?'

"I grinned big and said, 'Sir, you taught us to improvise.' That broke the ice.

"Yeah, so I called my wife and told her, 'Hey baby! I got a weekend pass!' We made it as far as the gate at Camp Pendleton and the Motel Six. That's where my son was conceived."

Cherries Sometimes Freeze—God Created the Marine Corps

Phil: "Let's talk about scout/sniper school. How was it having Gunnery Sergeant Carlos Hathcock as an instructor?"

Mike: "He's one of them. We had many. But Carlos was the one everyone talked about because he had the sniper experience and the reputation for his kills. In the Marine Corps, he was famous. Still is."

Phil: "I'd like you to really think about that series of classes. What was it they were trying to teach you? And then, in particular, you said to me that Carlos taught you things that saved your life. I want to hear some of those."

Mike: "Well, basically the job of a scout/sniper back then was reconnaissance and killing people. Learning reconnaissance skills. Hiding. If I don't want you to see me, you'll never see me. Enhancing our rifle skills."

Phil: "So you and Jonathan were all set up at the mansion waiting for this guy to show up that day."

Mike: "Yeah, yeah."

Phil: "And you had done these assignments before?"

Mike: "Yeah, that was my ninth kill. My ninth confirmed."

Phil: "I looked at your length of service in Vietnam. It was more than the standard thirteen months tour and then rotation home. Did you extend?"

Mike: "I volunteered for another tour. A lot of us back then did. There was no bonus. If you decide to stay, fine, sign a piece of paper, now you're on your second tour."

Phil: "Why wouldn't you go home?"

Mike: "I felt that I was saving lives. The people there, my fellow Marines, the South Vietnamese people were very appreciative. They understood why we were there. Had I not been wounded; I might have done a third too. I don't know. Carlos, he did, I think, four tours. Then he was burned really badly pulling guys out of a burning Amtrak."

Phil: "You know he died a young man?"

Mike: "Yeah, he died from complications from his time in Vietnam."

Phil: "What do you think it was?"

Mike: "I heard a blood disorder. He died at fifty-six.

"So, after the day would be done, and we were, you know, structured training was done, Carlos would come in and talk to us. He would share his experiences and what he did to stay alive. I learned more from him. I learned a lot, but I learned more from him than I think I did in school. He had a very kind, very soft, low, deep voice. And he wasn't very big."

Phil: "Do you think it happened at boot camp or maybe later that you decided that the Marine Corps is a pretty good thing?"

Mike: "I realized that the discipline I was being taught was a good thing. It kind of followed on my father's doctrine. My father was very strict, very precise with everything he did. That's what the Marine

Corps was, so I followed. In fact, I know when I graduated my platoon commander, S/Sgt. Henry, met my parents. He turns to Dad and says, 'Are you the gentleman that taught this Marine how to shoot?'

"Dad grins and goes, 'Yeah, I sure did.'

"S/Sgt. Henry says, 'You can come work for me anytime you want. I'll find a job for you.'

"Hey, I saw my dad one day in Nevada on horseback, the horse in a run, and he shoots three deer running away from us in three shots.

"He taught me how to shoot. How to lead. Like if you are going to shoot a deer, you aim at his nose when the deer is running. You know if you aim at the nose, that'll put the bullet right here at the heart. You only hit the heart because the deer is moving into the bullet's path."

Phil: "Your separation paper, your DD214, says 'physical disability without severance.' That's interesting."

Mike: "Yeah, they felt I was 100 percent. I was young and stupid and didn't challenge it. 'Cuz I knew I had a job at Miles and Son's waiting for me."

Phil: "What happened after you were released from Balboa and reported back to Camp Pendleton for reassignment?"

Mike: "They put me into what's called casual company because I didn't have an assigned unit.

The lieutenant pulls me in. 'Mr. Smith,' and I knew right there. He wasn't calling me by my rank. He says, 'I have some sad news for you. The Marine Corps is in a time of downsizing. We have to overall discharge fifty thousand troops in this phase. You're on the list.'

"I said, 'Well, why don't you just keep me here at Pendleton as a rifle instructor? I'm pretty good at what I do.'

"He goes, 'I'd love to. I'd do it in a heartbeat. You're one of the finest shots this military has ever seen. But I have my orders.'

"He hands me my discharge papers, and I think with the accrued leave I had on the books, it was like $2,800 bucks in cash. Back then, we got paid in cash. I don't know why, but my first call was to my old employer. I got the secretary—she and I were good friends—and she gave me to my boss.

"So this is all fate now; I say, 'I just got discharged from the military.' He didn't say great, thank you, or nothing. He just said, 'When can you be here?'

"Miles and Son's Trucking was in Mountain View near San Jose in the south bay area. This was a Thursday or Friday—I can't remember which, but I was like, 'I think I can be there Monday morning.'

Phil: "The Marine Corps has a reputation of elite service, an element of intangible commitment to something greater. I've noticed many times that Marines can have a cocky demeanor, almost bordering on arrogance both about themselves and even about other Marines."

Mike, "Yeah, so?"

Phil, "The Marine camaraderie, the Semper Fidelis, the whole feel of being dependent on each other, there for each other. With only a few, all have to step up. For me and most Marines I know, the Marine doctrine transcends other services in the sense of companionship, partnership, and team. A Marine would do anything for another Marine."

Mike: "I saw that in the compassion of S/Sgt. Henry. Outside the fact that he was very good, very tough, he had an enormous level of empathy and compassion. Once we earned the title Marine, everything changes. The drill instructors would call us everything. Girls, maggots, worms, everything. S/Sgt. Henry never said any of that. He left all of that to his subordinates. He'd let us come into his hut at night. Always low key, soft spoken, very seldom raising his voice.

Except now and again to offer a complimentary hoorah. All our drill instructors had good hoorahs. We just knew if we could do what he and S/Sgt. Dibble did, we would be okay. I admired them both."

Phil: "They were trying to prepare you. They knew you were going to Vietnam. They knew you were going to be in the middle of something soon. Most of you were going to be assigned to and joining Marine units at war."

Mike: "They told us more than once, 'We will prepare you to the point where the actual battle may not be as bad as what we're training.' When they explained it that way, all of a sudden, the training took on a new meaning. They would show us videos from the battle at Khe Sanh and how just a very few Marines withstood such a massive North Vietnamese attack.

"Marine grunt patrols, they were active. They would go out looking for trouble, trying to start a fight. I learned later our army guys did much the same. It was two or three platoons out hunting at night in the dark. That's when the NVA patrols were on the move. Or many times, they'd go out just before dawn. They were hunter/killer patrols. What they were about was trying to get our enemy in the open, out in the open field before they had the opportunity to bring their forces together for a larger attack.

"If the NVA had time, they would bring in enough troops to stage a mass attack at our camps. That can be overwhelming. The grunts went out looking for them to keep them off our bases and out where we had greater advantages. The grunts knew they had all kinds of support they could call on. They had artillery. They had fixed-wing air support. They knew they had helicopter support. They knew if things got really bad, they had Puff the Magic Dragon. Puff was an airborne arsenal. It was called Puff because it breathed down fire and smoke.

"Puff was often called on to come help out when our guys had a bunch of the enemy engaged and we were in trouble. Outnumbered. Puff was a specially equipped AC-47 Air Force transport. Slow moving transport-type airplane. Instead of cargo or troops, Puff had three six-barrel 7.62 miniguns mounted in open doors. Those miniguns were all mounted so that the barrels all were pointing out on one side. The pilots would lean the aircraft over in a banking turn so the spray of the miniguns favored that side as they circled the target zone and cut loose. When they fired those babies in unison from up above, any enemy force our guys had trapped on the ground would be rained on by lead. Thousands of rounds would rain down. From the view of grunts watching it stream, to us it looked like a dark gray downpour. Each gun is spraying three thousand rounds per minute. With three guns, nine thousand rounds are coming down. The spray puts a bullet in each and every yard of the target area. Very effective at reducing the threat, especially against enemy troops in large numbers. Grunts loved Puff. Hoorah.

"The North Vietnamese, their tactics were shoot and run, shoot and run. You could very seldom pin them down to a fight unless they had put together a flat-out ambush. If they had you in an ambush, that was trouble. The patrols were trying to catch them in the open before they got themselves massed up for an attack on our camps. Trying to keep them at bay.

All of our camps have escape backup plans. We had trenches on one side ready for our use in the event of an overwhelming assault. The NVA would hit a camp at night with huge numbers. Sometimes over a thousand. More than once, Puff was called to the rescue with our guys on the ground answering, "On our camp!" when asked where they should engage.

"Get this, the grunts' tactic when hit in the open. We attack. Get up and go at them. We all attack instantly and aggressively. We go at them so fast and so hard with so much fire they crumble and cover, and we shoot our way free. If we can't shoot our way free, we call in support on larger forces. Crazy. I mean, is that brave or crazy? It was so much safer doing what we did."

Phil: "But don't guys freeze?"

Mike: "Sometimes the new kids freeze. The cherries. If they get hit on an early patrol. Before they are seasoned. They don't mean to, but it happens. In a firefight, people are shooting at you, sometimes many people. Often, the chaos lasts for what can feel like some slow-motion extended time lapse. Many times, when bullets fly, each fraction of a moment feels very long. So much happens so fast, the brain can't process everything. If that happens, if a kid does freeze, one of the more weathered grunts will have to grab them or maybe even give him a little slap.

"That's one reason units only took a few new guys on any patrol. And they aren't allowed to bunch up. Got to have more combat-savvy guys than newbies. They had to learn to hold on to some ammo. It's easy to pucker up when bullets fly and keep reloading and keep firing when you are being shot at. But it's not good to go at it too fast and then be out of ammo. When you are out on patrol, it's just what you are carrying. Grunts carry M16s. You can carry three hundred, even four hundred rounds with the M16. In grunt units, that's a full load. Most guys would carry a full load.

"An interesting fact—at least I think this is close to true—US forces fire something like forty thousand rounds per enemy killed."

Phil: "What was Carlos's speaking style?"

Mike: "He was sharp. Real soft spoken but intense. He was very thorough, very detailed. He thought about survival like no one else.

If you'd just listened to him a bit, you'd know he's a very bright, very intelligent guy. And Carlos had very clean language."

Phil: "That doesn't seem typical of Marines. I knew some guys who couldn't start a sentence or say even a short phrase without using the f-word a minimum of three times."

Mike: "No, back then, it was very typical. Back then, really, we were not allowed to cuss. That's why when I hear stuff today, I just shake my head. I still can't watch some of what is out there today as entertainment. Too much filthy gutter mouth. Because, no, back then, there was no dirty word that came out of our mouths.

"The f-word was never used. A cuss word was never used. Because the attitude was, we are the Marine Corps. We are the protectors of the United States. We are to protect with honor and integrity. People are gonna know who we are. That was satisfying to me. So, like I say, the phrase, 'God created the Marine Corps to protect Americans, so they could worship Him.' That was the saying that was beat into our heads.

"Yeah, in my boot camp graduation book, there is a picture of us getting communion. Every Sunday when we were on base, we would go to church. The whole company. It was like this, we either raised our hands when asked if we wanted to go to church or we could stay at our hooch and do more prep for the coming week. We all raised our hands. Who wants to spend the whole weekend doing almost nothing all in one place? We knew we weren't getting liberty. Never going to happen. They marched us down, you know, and one Sunday, they gave us all last rites. God, and his powers, and his ability to save our souls, was part of our training. Part of our doctrine."

Death Slapped Me Right Square in the Face—Patton

Mike: "My father was a disciplinarian, a very strong disciplinarian. Which is strange because I'm a baby boomer, and most parents of the baby boomer generation coddled, and some even spoiled their kids. My dad was a total opposite. I mean, he wasn't abusive. I think I only got one or two spankings. But I remember those spankings, you know. If you weren't doing it right, he would show us how to do it right."

Phil: "You were with him for quite a big part of each day."

Mike: "Oh, yeah. And I have gratitude for him, even when my father in his later years was such a heavy drinker. I respected him.

"Unfortunately, I picked up on the drinking for a time and a lot of his other traits too. My father never showed emotion. It has taken me forty-plus years of marriage to show emotion. I just keep it all bottled up inside."

Phil: "Well, that's another thing to consider. You know, you have had to cope with all these experiences you went through."

Mike: "Yeah, not to me. I mean, part of what I saw in Carlos is that he was a person who ended up being very proud of what he had achieved. My feeling was very much deserved. So, yes, he did things with his rifle that they said he couldn't do. He had skills that were beyond what some thought fit the range of possible. He was a natural stalker, hunter. That was from his upbringing. That wasn't Marine Corps. The Marine Corps didn't teach him how to do that. His family did. He would talk about hunting back in the Ozarks.

"He was very patient. Oh, I wish I had his patience. I have a lot of patience, but he had ten times. What I mean is, he could go out and lay for thirty-six hours and never move except just a tiny bit in the dark of the night for water and his own personal needs. He'd be just waiting there for the right circumstance. If I was out more than six, eight hours, I had to really concentrate on not moving. It starts to hurt after too long. So yes, he was unique.

"You know, God has put, throughout history, certain people in certain places to get things done. Look at World War II. Patton is my hero. Yeah, look at the things he got accomplished. True, he was a rabble-rouser. Yes, he took chances. Yes, he had a big mouth. But when it came to battle, they knew he was the best we had. I've got his book by my bed, getting ready to read it again. *Patton: A Study in Command.* In the book, you know, he makes the comment about the first battle in North Africa. Famously, he shakes his fist in the air, 'Rommel, you magnificent bastard, I read your book.'

"Patton was a tactician. He had a sixth sense of knowing what the Germans were going to do and when they were going to do it. Even as inferior as our Sherman tanks were against the German tanks, he figured out tactics to get around that. He figured out that the German tanks, if hit from behind, could be taken down. Even the big Tiger tank, if you hit it from behind, you could take it out. Then Abrams, who our Abrams tank is named after, became the ultimate tactician of the Sherman tank. He destroyed a lot of German tanks. A lot of German tanks.

"I was raised to know if you study the past, you can predict the future. The past has a way of coming back and repeating itself. It's human nature. It may not be exactly alike but often it rhymes.

"One day, a stockpile of rounds may be important. Some don't want to believe that. But I do. I think it may happen yet in our lifetime. That's one of the things that concerns me long term."

Phil: "You've got three rings sitting right there."

Mike: "They are for bowling. Two are for perfect games, and one is for an eight hundred series. Before I was drafted, my aspirations were to become a professional bowler."

Phil: "You worked at a bowling alley as a kid. Did you play pinball games?"

Mike: "I played the Atari pinball game, Space Command. I got so good at it that they didn't have any more points to give me. Later, I bought one. Yeah, I was hooked on it. That and Missile Command. I got so good at it that nothing, nobody ever outscored me.

"I believe I likely would have been a pretty decent golfer too. Because of my hand-eye coordination. But I thought chasing a little white ball around...to me that was kind of stupid back then. You know, when I go bowling, the ball comes back to me.

"In those years, I had five perfect games and two eight hundred series. One of my proudest moments is I bowled a perfect game in front of my son. Over in Livermore. We both were bowling at the time and in a traveling league together. He was keeping score for us. I never did see that twelfth ball hit the pins. I just let it fly. I knew it was there. When it hit, I heard that sweet sound as pins fell, and I jumped up!"

Phil: "Was your boy a shooter?"

Mike: "He was. He was killed when he was twenty in a motorcycle accident."

Phil: "Oh, no! I'm so sorry."

Mike: "Yes, he was a shooter, and he was a good bowler too. He and I, we bowled together. He was a very good bowler."

Phil: "Was he with you at the time of his death?"

Mike: "No. He had just gotten married. He and his brother-in-law and their families were up in the hills dirt biking. His brother-in-law, Mike, and he collided. Mike had a compound fracture of his leg. Chris, my son, had internal injuries they couldn't see. So they all are working on and worried about Mike and his compound fracture. Finally, someone noticed Chris holding his chest. Inside, he had a severed artery from the impact. He died on the operating table at the hospital.

"But you know, it's funny. They call, no cell phones back then. So they call me, and they say, 'Your son is in surgery.' I went right over. When I walked in the hospital's front door, death slapped me right square in the face. I knew he was gone.

"That year, I lost Chris; I lost both my parents; my wife's brother; and my best friend, Ken; all died that year. I had a lot of people say, 'How can you believe in God?' It was a strain; it was a strain on my faith.

"I've been fortunate throughout my life; I've always seemed to have a mentor. I mean my dad, Staff Sergeant Henry, Carlos Hathcock, and many others."

Phil: "Did you have forced marches in boot camp?"

Mike: "Oh yeah. We had what's called route step. Five miles an hour doesn't seem that fast until you've done it a couple of hours and have a couple hours more to go. We marched from MCRD in San Diego up to Camp Pendleton. Back then graduates marched. We didn't ride a bus. It's got to be forty miles. We marched it in a little over ten hours. Marines call this a walk in the park. We didn't have our packs on; all our packs went on a truck. We're in our boots, cartridge belts, and two canteens. That was a pretty good hump."

Phil: "Did you carry two canteens in the field?"

Mike: "In Vietnam, I carried just one. Because in Vietnam, there's water everywhere. I mean, it could rain six inches in half an hour."

Phil: "Was it wet in January?"

Mike: "Not as much as later in the year but, yes, wet. Monsoon season is like June through October. That's when it's really, really wet. Beautiful country. I mean there is no more gorgeous, gorgeous green. And Laos, if it's even possible—just because of the way the forest is in the mountains—is even prettier than Vietnam."

Phil: "On this final mission, did you pass by any villages?"

Mike: "It was all jungle. No villages. On the other side, maybe a mile, three-quarters of a mile away is the mansion. We called it the mansion."

Phil: "Do you know your assignment's name?"

Mike: "I did but don't anymore. He was a colonel. And all I can say is he is the colonel in the North Vietnamese Army that orchestrated kids being strapped with grenades."

Phil: "Do you think Google has any history on this guy?"

Mike: "If there is, I'm the one that killed him."

Phil: "Did you ever Google Vietnam snipers?"

Mike: "No."

Phil: "There's a list of ten or twelve people out there. Hathcock and Sergeant Mawhinney are the two most successful.'

Mike: "Carlos had told us that Sgt. Mawhinney was one of the best shots he had ever coached. He was the Marine that one night; he was the forward outlook along a stream. A bunch of NVA wade into the stream, a fairly wide and deep stream to start coming across toward our guys. Well, he went at them last man first. He had his M1A1 with a starlight scope. Back then, night vision scopes weren't really that great. It was all green and had a lighter, shadowy look to anyone on the screen. And when the first round is fired, it goes a bit fuzzy. The light of the shot fired makes it fuzz out, kinda going whitish green for a very brief moment. But sixteen NVA troops with their rifles over their heads wade into the stream. In less than thirty seconds, sixteen dead North Vietnamese bodies floating down the stream.

"That convinced the rest of that NVA unit that there must be a whole bunch of American defenders. Started in the back of the stream. Sixteen headshots. Boom, boom, boom. Back of the pack, working his way forward. Those in front never saw who had fallen. He got them all.

"One of the famous stories told about Carlos has been made into a documentary. I've seen it on TV dozens of times. The one where Carlos shot an enemy sniper through his scope. Carlos, he would tell that story a lot. And he'd say, you know, 'I was within half a heartbeat of being dead. I know he had me in his scope. The fact that I saw his scope tells me he saw my scope. We both were ready. I just happened to be the one that squeezed the trigger first.'

"That shot went straight through the scope. That's right, the bullet went clean through. Then through the eye. Out the back of the skull with his brain. The glass of the scope was shattered and totally gone. The scope's casing was totally intact, untouched. Clean, straight through. Carlos said they had been stalking each other, switching positions in this valley among the mountains back and forth for a couple of days.

"Another story, he got a kill with a .50 caliber at something like two thousand yards. Carlos told us it was just dumb luck. He was just, you know, goofing off. He strapped a small scope on the .50 and went out there. Still, a long shot made. A lot of people don't recognize it, but it's still a lot of skill. He told us, 'When that guy stood up into the path of that round and then he drops, my jaw dropped too.'

"He said the guy just stood up right into the path of his round. A fifty doesn't fly that fast, maybe fired a half second earlier. And if a fifty round flying your way catches you anywhere, that's major damage. That's a big round. When you hold one in your hand, that thing is as long as your whole hand. The bullet part, the part that goes into flight, is as big around as your little finger and nearly as long. Huge. Major damage."

No Clicks—He Probably Saved My Life

Mike: "Carlos explained this to us one night. The common soldier in battle will never really see the person they shoot at. They only see up close if they are being overrun, when the battle has become hand-to-hand, close-quarters combat. Grunts work hard to avoid being overrun. On the other hand, the sniper is watching the face and expression of each of his targets through a high-power sighting scope and will see, up close and personal, the face and features of every person you kill. Snipers target specific individuals, predominately leaders. Snipers fire on their assignments from a hidden concealed position. Snipers fire when no one else is firing. Yes, seeing each person drop as the round impacts them in the head or face from your safe hide using sniper tactics can have a very dramatic effect on you mentally. It's military precision approved stealth and assassination of a proven American killer. It was only mostly safe when we were good enough to make the one shot one kill. That's where he told us, and I adopted his logic, that every time I was successful, I was saving lives. That kept me sane. Saving either Marines, army, South Vietnamese, or even sometimes North Vietnamese civilians. I was saving a life. He made the point over and over, one shot. If you want to survive, one shot.

"On top of that, he says, 'I know that God was sanctioning what I was doing.' I adopted that doctrine. God was with me.

"Then he says, and I thought this was a very interesting comment, he said that we're not trying to get Joe Schmuckatelli (Marine speak for the random trooper) who's carrying a rifle. We're after the guy that's making the decisions about who they go after. We are after the deadliest commanders. The ones that had killed many, many Americans. That's how they got on our list. He was absolutely right. Every assignment I had was a bad dude.

"Missions are voluntary. We could refuse. Most of us didn't want to take on spotters. They had a habit of getting killed. Carlos himself was vehement—no spotter. But things had evolved and now the regiment required us to use spotters. They were often aspiring snipers. Good shots, studying to be snipers. Spotters carry a weapon but are expected to never use it. We are on an assignment, not an engagement. We expect to make only one shot on every assignment. It's always good to have another set of eyes looking where you aren't, helping see more. But you had to teach them. How to camouflage, how to crawl, how to move without being seen, how to be quiet, how to look for trip wires and so forth. In some ways having a spotter is an advantage. Not in all ways. They slowed me down and together we made more noise.

"Camp Pendleton had areas that had no public access. In one of those areas, we had our own little Vietnam built on the back side of a mountain. All the grass, all the shrubs, everything that Vietnam had.

"We practiced hard on trip wires. The North Vietnamese were very big, very good at picking up discarded stuff and making booby traps. The Punji sticks, they are bad. Eventually, we got boots with steel bottoms. That helped quite a bit. Then they would take a used LAWS rocket tube and rig a grenade inside it. Pin pulled, spoon held in by the sides of the tube. Then they'd tie a trip wire across the path somewhere they thought we might walk through."

Phil: "Is this like fishing line?"

Mike: "Yeah, like very, very real light fishing line, almost impossible to detect. And they weren't dumb. They painted it green, you know, to match the terrain.

"These traps don't wear out. It hangs there for a long time. We trained, when you felt it on your leg, the wire, you're not going to get...you're not going to get away. Number one, we were trained just to dive for the deck. Let the blast go over the top of you.

"Unfortunately, I got hit going down, and Jonathan, a half a step behind, he didn't have time to get down. Caught him across the lower abdomen."

Phil: "What did he say?"

Mike: "He goes, 'Oh, shit.'

"I'm saying, 'I'm sorry, I'm sorry, I'm sorry.' But sometimes things happen. I put a tourniquet on my leg. He was in a good amount of pain. Gut shots are very painful. Very, very painful."

Phil: "I'm guessing not many words are spoken once you are in-country."

Mike: "It is all hand signals. Because out there, the voice travels. Not necessarily that humans hear it, but a dog would hear it. They've got a heck of a lot better hearing than we do."

Phil: "You said you ate the local food."

Mike: "At the briefing, they would have a prepared manila folder with details of the assignment. Often a picture of the individual, location, time, place, and a brief about this person. Knowing where we were going, I'd go to a South Vietnamese counterpart in our camp and tell him in general terms where I'm going, then ask, 'How do people there eat?' This guy, not very tall, gets a big smile. 'Okay, you eat this, this, and this.' So ten days prior, I started eating that stuff. Lots of fish, how it was cooked or boiled. Spices, insects, grasses, roots, and a bit of rice.

"That's one thing Carlos said. It's got to be ten days to get all of your usual GI stuff out of your pores. When you're out there and you're sweating like a pig because you are going to, those Ghillie suits are very warm, you want your sweat to smell as they smell—normal. And it worked. I had a Rottweiler walk right over the top of me one night."

Phil: "How high is the adrenaline when you're out in the field? It must be pretty high almost all the time."

Mike: "No, actually my adrenaline when I was wounded was very high. But prior to that, we were trained how to relax and how to lower our bodily functions. My heartbeat could go down to forty beats a minute. That was something that was a sort of survival tactic."

Phil: "Wow, that's low. Are there creatures or critters that get you or get in your way?"

Mike: "Snakes. But out in the grass, most snakes will move away just from the vibration on the ground of our weight. Sometimes, especially at night if you are lying very still a snake will come alongside. I never had an issue with ants or bugs much. We had black grease on, so the bugs would tend to leave us alone. The grease was to blacken the face. Totally black, so you couldn't see us."

Phil: "You said you didn't take food because this was an in-and-out, less than two-day mission, right? And only one canteen because water was everywhere?"

Mike: "We took iodine pills to drop in the canteen when we filled it to make it drinkable. Sometimes a little diarrhea but usually not bad."

Phil: "But you couldn't sneak out for a leak break if you needed to?"

Mike: "Once we were in a location, you stay there. If you had to go, you just went in your pants. I would stop drinking any liquid and try to take a last leak before we left the jungle. Once there, you don't stand up to take a leak because that created motion, and you would make some noise. So, you would lay on your side, just kind of letting it dribble out. These are little tricks of the trade that Carlos taught me. Little things that keep you alive."

Phil: "I've always thought it was the motion that gives a sniper away."

Mike: "Sometimes. But the ear, too, will pick up motion. The ear, once trained—you'd be surprised at what you hear. It's just like, we were trained that the deadbolt makes a certain click. That's very similar to the click of a rifle bolt being closed. Growing up, my teen-aged daughter could never figure out how we knew what time she got home. Once she'd hit that lock, and it went click, I was awake. These are things you live with the rest of your life. I'm always trying to be facing the door, or toward a window.

"The actual experiences that I gained from Carlos were invaluable. I know it probably saved my life. Three or four times over. You know, how to stay concealed, how to move, how to not be smelled. Those are things that you didn't learn in the classroom. They are things you learn from someone who has been there. You never flipped the end of your scope up until you were ready to shoot. You shielded it with your hand if the sun was in front of you. The sun could glance off of it, create a glare, a reflection of light, and someone could pick it up. You've got people out there looking all the time, so you have got to be invisible."

Phil: "In a pair, like you were with Jonathan, you took turns on working the scan?"

Mike: "Usually, thirty minutes was what we would do. He used a field glass; I used my scope. But that's only when you are looking for targets. If you have a specific target, that really isn't necessary because you know what your specific target is. Sometimes, like we were, you're just waiting for him to show up. Sometimes, we waited, and he never shows up.

"Now, Jonathan this time spotted the truck, the convoy, long before I did because he was working his scan. He was on my right side. He turns to me. He mouthed, 'dust' and pointed. I knew exactly what he meant. I had my rifle in my shoulder, and I saw the vehicle coming in my scope. I'm focused on the vehicle. He's concentrating on the building where this dude is going to go and the guards that are out there. He's looking for anything strange happening. He's going to complement me and pick that up.

"I had figured in my mind roughly seven hundred yards. But Jonathan—because we didn't have range finders, if we wanted to know the wind, we'd take a handful of grass and drop it. Jonathan says 680 yards. So okay, fine.

"He's looking, and he twirls his finger pointing towards his nose. He's telling me, 'Looks like the wind is blowing toward us.'

"It's early in the day. Light breeze coming, it feels just like he said, right in the face. Our position was pretty level with the mansion. I didn't have to add an adjustment for being higher or lower, just for the longer-than-usual distance."

Phil: "Talk about arriving in Vietnam."

Mike: "It took a day; we flew into Saigon. Then it took a day and a half for me to hitch a ride on a convoy up to my camp. The camp was not too far from Khe Sanh."

Phil: "What was the base name?"

Mike: "It was a number, not a name. Not a base, a camp. Camp 43. A lot of camps just had numbers unless, of course, there was a nearby town.

"When I first arrived, I was brought in; the sergeant introduces me to people. There were two of us that came in together. I can't remember the other guy's name because we never talked. We just kept to ourselves. And this is where I met up and was married to Jonathan. Jonathan had not gone to sniper school. He wanted to. He had applied for it but had not yet been accepted. He had gone to his platoon sergeant, applied for sniper school, and then asked to be assigned to help snipers assigned to the unit. He was hoping that one day he'd get approved for the school. His application was pending. For the most part, unless I, his sniper, deemed he should have a long-range weapon, he would carry an M16. And then he had his monocular scope. It was not a rifle-mounted scope but a more powerful twenty-power freehand sighting glass. It was shaped a bit oblong. He could use that for spotting things. That's why they call them 'spotter.'"

Phil: "Had Jonathan been spotting for other snipers?"

Mike: "I think once. Because he had just gotten there also. We spent a couple of days going over my routine. I said, 'I'm not trying to be arrogant; just forget your routines. Now, you're going to be going out with me. We do things my way. Otherwise, you're going to get killed.' He had no clue about the food or anything like that at first.

"When I got my first assignment, I went to the lieutenant. 'Sir, this is the area I'm going into. I've got to start eating their food.'

"He kind of looked at me cross-eyed."

"I said, 'You do want me to come back alive, right? You know this is what Carlos taught me.'

"The lieutenant says, 'Oh, you had Carlos?'

"'Yeah, I did.'

"Lieutenant—'Okay, what do you need?'

"So Jonathan started learning from me what Carlos had taught me."

Phil: "Were they willing to have that much patience?"

Mike: "Well, a sniper always had the right to refuse any mission. Flat out, no questions asked. Just, I'm not going. In fact, that one about Mawhinney—three other snipers turned the assignment down. Watching that river is like guard duty. It's not our job. He says, 'Yeah, I'll go, but I'm taking this rifle instead of the Remington.' Damn good that he did, or he'd probably be dead."

Phil: "What rifle did he take?"

Mike: "The M1A1, M14. Importantly, with a twenty-round clip. The Remington had five in the clip plus one in the chamber. Bolt action. Those two are both sniper rifles. The Remington is a precision, longer range rifle. Good out to about fifteen hundred yards. The M1A1, at one thousand yards, you're pushing the envelope.

"I used my M1A1 on most assignments. I got to be better and better with it.

"We practiced and got good at adjusting for the conditions. If we could see a flag or something, trees moving, grass waving, then I may not hold dead center. I may go off, too, just a bit in a breeze or even a bit more if the wind might be stronger. One day at Camp Pendleton, the wind was blowing so hard, I was shooting my buddy's target to hit mine. Those are things we were taught to do. Mother nature will tell you where the wind is if you pay attention to it.

"Now, a good spotter. If you have a good spotter, and you have to fire more than one round, your first bullet, in its travels, will leave a vapor trail. A good spotter will pick it up and help you make the appropriate adjustment. That's one of the spotter's primary duties, to see the path of the round, to see its impact point.

126

"We never needed a second round."

Phil: "Estimating distance must be hard."

Mike: "Yeah, we used to practice. We'd go out, and Carlos would point. From here to that tree, how far? You'd better be within twenty-five yards, or otherwise he makes you practice over and over. You learn to look at things and judge distance. With my logical, square mind, it was not difficult for me."

Phil: "Those scopes you used have adjustments for wind and elevation, right?"

Mike: "Yes, there is a bar that you can go up fifteen, maybe twenty clicks actually. I was taught by Carlos—don't mess with your scope. Get it set up for four hundred yards. Beyond that, you just hold a little to the right, a little to the left, a little up, a little down. So know your range, know the ballistics of your weapon. Okay, say if you've got a two-degree downhill. You've got to figure, instead of shooting directly at your target, aim a little lower because the bullet's going to rise. That way, the rising round will hit where you want. This is the science that he was a master at, an absolute master. We had to memorize it. Don't mess with your scope, mess with your aiming point. If you mess with your scope, you're turning a knob, and it's making a click. A click can get you killed. Besides, it takes time to turn the knob. Often you don't have time. Adjust the aiming point, save time, complete the mission.

"Carlos had a way. Yes, he was very soft spoken. When he addressed you by your last name, all was good. But if he used your rank, you best listen up 'cause you're in trouble.

"It was little things I learned from him. My dad was pretty much the same way. My rifle, my hunting rifle, the six millimeter, it had a three to nine Leopold scope on it. I just set it to nine and adjusted my aim. Same idea."

I Still Cry—At the Wall

Mike: "There's what's called snap shooting or slap shooting. Like, if I have three guys coming at me, I'm going bang, bang, bang. There is no time to aim. It's point and shoot. If you know your weapon and you are good enough, your point and shoot can be very accurate, very effective.

"If you have time to aim with a rifle, breathe and exhale halfway. At that point, your rifle stops moving. You start your smooth, steady squeeze. Ideally, you never want to know when that weapon discharges. It wants to be a surprise every single time. Then you're not jerking at the trigger. You're not anticipating anything.

"But in a crisis, where you've got a few seconds to fire ten rounds, it's what's called slap.

"The M14 was the first rifle our troops used in Vietnam, and at the time, it was the standard service weapon, the one everyone carried. The consensus was it was too heavy. You couldn't carry enough ammunition; it weighs you down. That's when the M16 was developed. Its caliber was smaller, 5.56. Being smaller, rounds were lighter. Grunts could carry four, five hundred rounds. With the M14, because of the larger-caliber 7.62, if you carried two hundred fifty rounds, you've got a lot more weight.

"Grunts loved the performance of the M14; they didn't want the M16. They didn't like the lighter round, the lighter killing force. It was harder to knock charging troops down. And it looked so different with its pistol grip and vented barrel shroud. But it was so much lighter.

"Later, the manufacturer of the M14, in their effort to compete with the new, lighter M16, developed what's called the SOCOM M14. They shortened the barrel, and they lightened it up with a composite fiber stock. Our standard-issue M14s had walnut stocks. They were heavy. That composite stock lightened it up like four pounds. Had they done the same with the M14 earlier, before the M16 came on scene, I don't think the M16 would have ever been adopted. If it would have, it would have taken years to take hold.

"Early on, the M16 was more prone to jams. And that was a bit ironic because the designer, Stoner, had been out there telling everybody it was a jam-proof weapon. A lot of good soldiers died because it jammed. Stoner quickly engineered a fix to the jamming, and the M16 became the primary US infantry weapon. It's the automatic version. Its cousin is the AR-15, the nonmilitary semiautomatic version that is so popular with gun people, even today.

"We were trained, you fire your weapon, you get back, you clean it, period. They all had said, hey, the M16, don't worry about cleaning it. They didn't even issue cleaning kits. Well, it was very weird. With the humidity and the mud and all the stuff of Vietnam, it jammed.

"By the way, that's why the Soviet AK47 is so popular throughout the world. It's got such loose tolerances that it won't jam. Of course, the tradeoff is it's not as accurate. I'll stand at five hundred yards and let you shoot at me with an AK47. You might hit me once in thirty shots, where the M14, even out to one thousand yards, I got you every time.

"I've shot the M16. It's good out to three hundred, three hundred fifty yards. Pretty accurate. But that little bullet is very prone to wind. Very, very prone. It's only a sixty-grain round.

"Vietnam forever changed my life. I still suffer today. I can watch a TV program, I'll hear a certain sound, a tone, a certain word, and out of nowhere, I'm in my recliner blubbering. A big tough Marine sobbing. It just comes over me, out of nowhere.

"After all these years, I still cry. Sometimes at strange moments, strange things.

"When we came home from Vietnam, we had tomatoes and eggs thrown at us. All kinds of stuff. Called names, sworn at, the whole bit. Coming home, for many of us, we were there just a few days ago in the jungle fighting with guys who would be at your side, defending your back. Guys were hit. Wounded, some dying. Just a few days ago, we were hunting and killing enemy troops. They were hunting and killing us. We had been there and survived. It felt so great to be coming home. One tour is a long time to be away. Many of us stayed beyond one to help out. We had gotten good at what we were doing. We are at war for our family, our home, our brothers, and each other. We felt we had been doing war with honor. Being men of honor. Being Marines, being good Americans. Doing what we were trained to do. We knew we had gotten good at it. We were proud of each other. Proud of our skill. Proud to have survived. Now we are home. So grateful and relieved to be home. And then this disrespect and rudeness from the dudes sitting safe at home. Even from some of the women. Some of them have mouths worse than the guys. Made you wonder.

"One thing Carlos told us: you don't need to brag about what you are doing. The label 'sniper' tells people you kill people. He says, 'If you get someone out there that's bragging about what they did, they probably never did it. The quiet ones are the ones you've got to pay attention to.'

"There is no disconnect between God and war. Read the Bible clear through. There's more violence in the Bible than all our wars combined. Look at the hero King David. He was a bad person in so many ways, but he loved God with all his heart.

"It was good that I went right back to work after discharge. I wanted to be busy to help me keep from thinking about where I had been. What I had been doing. It helped having things to do that were productive, right, and clear cut. My work made it much easier to avoid dwelling so much on what I had just been through."

Phil: "Did you have an experience with those dogs?"

Mike: "I never had an altercation with one. The North Vietnamese predominately use Rottweilers up north. Those dogs were good. Carlos beat it into our heads—if you can't have at least seven days to eat whatever you need to eat to get it into your pores, don't take it. Let the assignment go by. I was in the middle of a field with my Ghillie suit, lying flat. One just walked over me and kept going. I never saw his master; he just kept walking. I wasn't going to move an inch, just lay as still as I could, listening and listening.

"The Ghillie suit is a hooded jacket and loose overall pants that you tuck yourself into over the standard utility uniform for camouflage. When you have it on right, only trained eyes might see you. No, not named after anybody. I heard 'Ghillie' is Scots Gaelic and means 'young servant.' I don't know why. The Brits first used them in the Second Boer war. The ones we wore had shades of greens and browns that blended in with the terrain we were operating in. With it on, you could look directly at me and not see me.

"The suits are a sort of burlap fabric and made with pockets and sleeves to let us mix in branches, leaves, and grasses pulled from surrounding plants. Naturally, wearing Ghillies on top of utilities is warm, very warm. One of the primary reasons for the food was so that when you are in the suit sweating, you don't smell weird. Jonathan helped me put on mine; I'd help him into his. As we get closer to our hide, we'd grab some of the natural foliage to stick into it. Each of us put together our own suit. That is, we selected what to pull from the surrounding trees, brush, bushes, and grass to add to our outfit.

"Body alignment refers to the idea of always positioning yourself so that your rifle is aligned with your spine. You want the rifle butt in your shoulder to feel the same each time and to return in its recoil to the same posture after each round is fired. Your cheek on the stock—always in the same spot. Your eyes' distance from the scope always the same. Any variation in position of your eye can cause your aim to be off and your shot to miss. We worked at and were good at making the sight picture the same each time. Eye relief is the same idea. Getting your eye in the same direct line behind the scope, same distance, same elevation, same comfortable spot. With practice, you can get a feel for having it locked in. We wanted that spot to be the automatic spot, every time.

"You had to have a good, solid grip. You don't want to squeeze. If you squeeze too hard, you can start to tremble, to shake. Just a firm, a good firm grip. You become one with the rifle. They used that term, 'one with the rifle,' all the time. We got where we could pop the rifle right to the spot on our cheek.

"You want the crosshairs in the scope to be crisp and the head of your target to be a bit fuzzy. If the view of your target's head is clear and your crosshairs are fuzzy, you don't have the right sight picture, and you will miss.

"It's just like deer hunting. You learn to lead a running deer. Same thing if a guy is walking away. You aim a bit ahead, taking into account pace, distance, and elevation.

"A lot of the hunting technique came from my dad. The details, the patience—Carlos put a lot of effort into being good and teaching us how to be good. How to survive.

"In Vietnam, we would stay sharp for our missions by taking some practice rounds around our base before we went out. Just to make sure we had the rifle set up for the mission and had our eyes set for distance and current weather.

"One exercise we did all the time was to practice our trigger squeeze with an empty weapon. You stand a dime out at the end of the barrel at the v in the vanes of the front sight. If you can pull the trigger all the way to a click with a spent round chambered and the dime stays on your sight, you've got it down. The empty shell in the chamber is there to protect the firing pin from taking a ding as we practiced. Keeping the dime from falling as you gently squeeze requires a firm, steady grip. With the dime out at the end of your barrel, it's not easy. It takes a lot of practice. Many shooters can't do it at first. It's an acquired skill. Takes time, patience, and practice. Good shooters don't drop dimes.

"When you are positioned correctly, the rifle is going to come right back to where it should be for a second shot. Same thing with the discharge. With a semi auto weapon, you don't have to worry about it. The rifle self-ejects. If you are using a bolt action, you clear it, and you are ready for your second shot. It should not take but a fraction of a second to eject and reload. Once you squeeze, your thumb comes up and then back, and then you're loaded. No wasted motion.

"Carlos beat into our heads, you're not out there to enjoy what you do. If you start enjoying it, you better get the hell out of there.

You're going to get yourself killed and maybe someone else killed. You're there to save lives. A lot of people don't understand that you are taking lives, but you are there to save lives. You're there to save Marines, other Americans, South Vietnamese soldiers, and civilians. You're disrupting the entire battle plan of the enemy. One sniper could, at times, do more damage than a whole company of soldiers. If you take out the right person, cut the head off the snake, the rest of the body doesn't know what to do.

"Silencers came out of Vietnam. They were first developed for the .22 pistol. The sole purpose was to get rid of the sentry dogs. They called them 'hush puppies.' Military gallows humor. But, you know, if they send a dog out and it doesn't come back, they can become pissed and try to come find you. Carlos cautioned us to think twice before stirring the hornets' nest.

"One thing that Carlos also taught us was if there was animal dung out there, lay on it or next to it. You know, a turd is going to help camouflage you. Maybe save your life. He says, 'Yeah, if there is a fresh pile, it will help you not stand out. You don't want to stand out in any way, not in any shape or form.' I think the longest I had to lay out in the field was a bit over eight hours.

"We had a backpack for the Ghillie suit. It would roll up into a little pouch. We wore a combat vest over our utilities. It had pockets for our magazines, shoulder mounting points for our K bars, and room for what we needed for the mission. The vest is similar to what a police SWAT guy would wear or even a bit like those vests used by fly fishermen. I was carrying four loaded twenty-round magazines on my vest. My cartridge belt had my canteen, my .45, and two seven-round magazines for the .45.

"On this mission, we didn't carry anything to eat. It was an in and out, one day, a day and a half max mission. We knew if we ate a Hershey bar, we could smell like a Hershey bar. So we didn't take anything but what we needed to get the job done. We both took a final smallish drink of water before we left the jungle. We didn't want to have to pee, and we knew we would be sweating off moisture in our Ghillie suits.

"That's another reason for eating their food before. If you pee and your pee smells different, the dogs can get you. Then you're dead. Usually when we came back from a mission, we were dehydrated. We'd want to drink water, beer, Jack Daniel's, whatever we could get our hands on.

"Jonathan was like my long-range perimeter safety net. It was around 0700; I was looking at the mansion, trying to envision where this guy might be when I could take the shot. Where would his car stop? If not there, where else? Would he get out and walk toward the front, or might he turn the other direction and take a step toward the corner? I wanted to play out multiple scenarios in my head, so that no matter what actually happens, we've got a firing solution for it. That's what a spotter gives you: time to prepare and have distances, best alternate solutions, and optimum positioning for whatever plays out.

"Jonathan sees the dust. We both are eyes on the vehicle as it rolls to a stop. The colonel jumps out, and there's a porch ahead of him. Maybe three or four steps up, I'm on him with my scope from the time he gets out, on the back of his head as he walks toward the porch. He turns back to the car, barking at his guys down by the vehicles. I know I have ten to maybe thirty seconds. I've got my window. I squeeze. I'm watching him, keeping my aim firm but loose. I see his motion come to a pause. He gives them a stare. Now is my time. I just flowed with him, right through the scope.

"It's similar to hunting, like I did as a kid. A different kind of target. Instead of four legs, two. What I got from my father, along with from

Carlos, made me what I was. There's no question in my mind, had I not had the father I did, I doubt I would have become a scout/sniper."

Phil: "I read a story about a police sniper. He had to take out a guy. He said when he fired, the dude's head exploded. Is that what happens?"

Mike: "If it hits at the right angle, and it depends on the bullet. If you've got a hollow point, yeah, the head will explode. If you hit where the skull is the thickest, the head will explode. If you hit where the skull is thinnest, it just goes through. It does make a big hole coming out. Yeah, I had a few heads explode."

Phil: "And, of course, your target drops?"

Mike: "Yeah, they cease to exist. I've told a lot of people that saw combat, if you've got an M16 or whatever and you're shooting fifty, a hundred, maybe two hundred yards away, you don't see the bullet hit what you are shooting at. You don't even always know for sure it was your shot. If it was, you don't see close up the damage it does. I had to see every time. That is a big difference. It affected us. And spotters have an even more personal view because first their glass is stronger magnification than my scope, and the recoil of the weapon takes the scope off the target for just at the moment when the weapon fires. I could see as my target fell, but Jonathan could see him get hit. Not an easy job.

"The enemy, in the night attacks especially, often were so high on opium, you could kill them, and they won't know they were dead. They'd smoke it all day. And then they'd attack. Seriously, so many of them were high out of their minds on the stuff. They came attacking with cloth ties around their arms and legs at strategic spots to mini-mize blood loss when they got hit. The story is that our troops were loaded all the time. That's not true. Our guys would get drunk, sure, and some got loaded, but only a very few and mostly when they were not on the frontline. On the front line, no, there was very few of them.

"Booze was easy to get. Marijuana was easy to get. But in combat, we had very few, maybe 1 or 2 percent, because everyone immediately knew if you were impaired. No one likes having a partner that might make you vulnerable. Often guys who went out impaired went home dead.

"I would drink after missions when I was back at the camp. Sure. Beer, Jack. If I could get my hands on a bottle of Jack, you know, a pint. Yeah, I would drink it. Sure, just so I could go to sleep. It's not easy to sleep when you are all keyed up. Adrenaline and killing will keep you up at night.

"There was no prejudice in the Marine Corps. If you did the work, if you could pull your weight, everyone was the same. S/Sgt. Henry used to say, 'I don't care if you are black, blue, green, gray, brown, yellow, as long as you could do the job. We all bleed red.' After we had been there for a bit, we knew what he meant."

"I did come out of the service with a little prejudice against the Vietnamese. Okay, to be more honest, I'd say more than a little. Because of what I saw over there."

Phil: "I keep thinking, after you took the shot that got your guy, that they would be chasing you. Did you ever see or hear anyone?"

Mike: "No. When we had made it maybe a hundred yards or so into the jungle, we weren't going to be found. We got out of our Ghillie suits, put them in our backpacks, took a whiz, and started running. I'm just ahead, Jonathan is right with me. We are moving, getting away, and going toward our extraction. We were going out on a different route than when we came in. Carlos taught us you never come out on the path you went in. They could be tracking you.

"Yeah, the guards panicking helped us get away. After he dropped, they didn't know where the bullet came from. With the terrain, there were instant echoes. Each sentry heard the shot from a different direction. They were just spraying the air. We crawled back into the jungle in a minute or two. Once in the jungle, we felt safe. We were running. I was planning to stop about a half mile in. Then we could evaluate if anyone is coming. Really listen to see, do we hear anything? We were in the jungle only about a minute when the grenade went off."

Phil: "Do you think you were knocked out for a moment?"

Mike: "No, I never lost consciousness. Jonathan didn't either. He was in a lot of pain. He tried very hard not to even moan or groan. I could just see the intense pain in his face. I still see that even now. He didn't want to make any noise because noise can kill us. Noise was against our rules. I put a tourniquet on my leg, then gave him the morphine. I could see he was a mess. I bandaged him as best I could. I got his poncho out. I just wrapped it around his middle. I didn't take anything off. I just wrapped him real tight, trying to put pressure on his left side. He was awake and still in agony. As soon as I gave him the second morphine, he kinda went to la-la land. I had my poncho over him, wrapping him onto my back, and I pulled the sleeves under my belly, tied them together around my chest, and now we were ready to go. Thankfully, he was a smaller guy, probably 145 pounds, five six. I'm 165 and five ten."

Phil: "Helicopters can't stay overhead all that long. They have a bit more than two hours' flight time when they are fully fueled. So they've got maybe an hour and a half or two hours to be on station, then they need to go back to refuel. These three pickup times—it most likely was a different crew or crews than the guys that put you in. You guys were dropped off just after midnight. Each extraction time a helicopter came on station looking for you could have been the same aircraft and crew. Could have been some other."

Mike: "There were crews that volunteered to fly inserts and extractions."

Phil: "Yes, and back at the squadron, the flight operations people are assigning missions to aircrews. Everyone knows everyone. Flight surgeons and corpsmen are attached to squadrons. The crews include the two pilots, the crew chief, and the corpsman. Four guys go out to get you two. The crews coming back from the early times that you didn't make would have come back empty and reported your no-show. That meant the next extraction time was a go. New crews going out would know. Each one would be more alert. Yours isn't the only act in town, these crews would have had other missions to accomplish – resupply ammo, food, people, or pull someone else out. Looking for you is a primary mission but the others had to be done too. "

"That final extraction flight may have already been on station for some time when you heard them and popped your smoke. These air crews knew you two as the crazy-ass snipers that they put out into a field somewhere and then come back a day or two later to pick you up. This time was the first time you had missed your first pickup time ever. Then you missed your second. And now you were late for the final extraction time. 'Where are those spooky, sniper guys? Did someone get them?'

"You know, these aviation Marines appreciated what you did. And they thought you were crazy brave and putting yourselves at great risk to do what you set out to do. Two grunts going out alone to change the battle. Risking all for the mission. Saving someone else's butt. They would stay looking for you as long as they could."

Mike: "Were we risking our lives? Yes, we did. But we didn't think of it that way. I never thought, 'I'm risking my life.' I have a job to do.

I've been trained to do it. I've been trained how to, with one round, let more people survive."

Phil: "Your final assignment, this guy was very senior."

Mike: "Yes, he was the most senior for me ever. Most assignments were equivalent to our first sergeant or captain, something like that. Maybe a lieutenant. This guy, when they told me that he was the one, what he was doing, it set me off. It was the fact he was using kids. I volunteered to take the mission."

Phil: "I'm thinking that this final mission is vivid in your mind because you have retold it many times over the years."

Mike: "No, I haven't told the story much. Maybe to a half dozen people. I've never told it in the detail we have discussed. It's incredibly well ingrained for me and my mind because Jonathan died. That has been, continues to be, the bad point for me. It's hard. That is why I couldn't get this out of my head, off my mind, out of my heart. I have relived it many times. Every day I think of him and how his life might have unfolded. It's still very painful."

Phil: "It must be so hard to have done all you did and still end up losing him. Did you try to contact his family?"

Mike: "I was told that job wasn't my job. It's one of the first things I asked about with my doctor in Balboa. Like, as soon as I could talk. He tells me there is a special casualty detail in the service to notify the family, offer support, and comfort. He said to me, 'No, Corporal, it's not your job.'"

Phil: "I knew a guy who had that duty. A lieutenant. He had the look of a guy that could handle doing that. He said it was tough. Some next of kin are wives, some parents, some brothers, and sisters. He said, 'They always knew as soon as they saw us drive up why we were there.' Most were considerate, kind, heartbroken, and thoughtful. Many cried. He tried not to cry. At times, he wasn't successful.

Some were angry and rude in their grief. Some yelled and screamed profanity and spit out evil, demeaning ugly words. He said in those cases, he left quickly. Otherwise, he stayed until the right moment. As long as they wanted."

Mike: "It really upset me that I couldn't talk to his family. I've blamed myself every day since he died. Why were we running? Maybe if we had just kept walking, we would have seen and avoided the trip wire.

My wife and I went to DC and the Wall in 2013. I always wanted to go but didn't want to go. So many names. I found the 1970 panel. I found Jonathan's name; they have his date of death correct. I reached up; my hand touched his name.

"I felt a sense of relief. It was a spiritual moment for me. I felt Jonathan's presence. He let me know he is at peace. I stood there in my sorrow and grief forty-three years later, sixty-four years old, like it was yesterday.

"I prayed inside. I touched the Wall again. It was a moment. Tight throat, moist eyes. I felt a connection to every one of the 57,939 names. Something like 2,700,000 plus Americans spent some time serving in Vietnam. Many of those have come to the Wall to see a friend.

"I had tried to bury my emotions. The Marine Corps taught us to bury our emotions. Emotions in battle will kill you. You have to rely on your training, rely on your skills. You don't let your emotions get involved because you'll be dead. I let that training bury my emotions way too long, way too well. I have lived with the guilt of Jonathan's death every day since.

"The next day, after being at the Wall, we went out to Arlington to the Tomb of the Unknown Soldier. We stood watching with a whole group of strangers in silence and awe as the sparkling honor guard marched out their post for quite some time. It was a thing of beauty.

Precise. Inspiring. Awesome and moving. For me, spiritual. Again. You could see why they call them honor guard.

"As I stood there, admiring the dignity, the respect, I had a sense again of God's presence. His forgiveness and grace. His peace. His love."

TRUE RUMORS—SGT. MAJOR PLUMLEY

Phil: "The very first time they sent you out into the field, you're in Vietnam for the first time, you weren't thinking, 'What the heck am I doing?'"

Mike: "I never thought that. Carlos took that out of us in training. He says, 'You're there because you want to be. You're there because you're trained to be.'"

Phil: "What you are telling me is that you probably were safer than an infantry guy by a fairly large margin?"

Mike: "I was so much safer than the average guy, the average grunt. We were trained to a point where we didn't even have to think about what we were going to do."

Phil: "How many times had you and Jonathan operated as a team?"

Mike: "I think three times before this. We would check each other's paint. Face grease, like makeup only much darker. And I had a couple of different spotters. They got assigned and rotated by the command. Many spotters felt safer with a sniper than doing line duty. Jonathan was one of those guys, and he followed my commands well. He was very quiet in the jungle. That's one of the things that I liked a lot about him. We understood each other's hand signals. Even though I didn't want him there, I was comfortable with him there. I had several assignments with no spotter and some with other spotters. Which spotter I was paired with was kind of random. On this assignment, I was going to ask for him when they told me he was already on standby.

"Most of the time, we aren't walking side by side. That's too big a target, right? Usually, I'm in front and he's in back, but occasionally, he'd take the point. And we'd try to stay within five yards of each other. Whoever was following had to keep a visual on the point all the time. The jungle could get thick. You learn to look at what way the grass is growing. Which way is it leaning? Which way the wind is blowing it. You try not to walk against the grain. Unless someone is within fifty yards of us, you're not going to hear us."

Phil: "Scope?"

Mike: "Mine was a fixed nine-power Redfield. I don't know why the military was so chintzy back then on their scopes. The rifles were good, but their scopes were terrible. It had a focus ring. It had adjusting dials I never used because of Carlos. Its power allowed you to see the whole target area and your individual's full profile, whereas today's scopes with more power let you put the crosshairs right on the head."

Phil: "How the heck did you get your direction after you went down?"

Mike: "I had my compass. I always carried it. I knew I had to head a certain degree on the compass to be near our drop-off LZ. I'd pick a landmark in that direction, move to it, pick another, do the same all the way out."

Phil: "You tied the rifles to your shoelace?"

Mike: "My rifle to my right boot. Same thing for him."

Phil: "And you're crawling through jungle grass. Doesn't the rifle get hung up?"

Mike: "Sometimes, yeah. I'd yank it. I don't think I had to pull my knife and cut anything free. I don't remember doing that. It may have happened."

Phil: "How did you get your sleeves off your shirt? You said you cut your sleeves off?

Mike: "I used my K bar knife. My knife was razor sharp. I had stopped to take a breather and to check how Jonathan was doing. This was at the wet muddy spot where I dug up some mud."

Phil: "And you used those pieces of material you cut off to bandage, to help bandage Jonathan. What were you trying to do?"

Mike: "The field bandages I had used had become saturated. They weren't doing any good anymore. I buried them in the mud so they wouldn't be found. I used the shirt sleeves to put a band around his waist. I had to take off his shirt to cut the sleeves off and then put it back on. Same for me. I wanted pressure on the wounds to keep the bleeding down. He had taken lots of shrapnel. I tried everything I could to stop the bleeding."

Phil: "So when you use the powder, that stops some of the bleeding, and then you try to bind it to get pressure. You're trying to hold that wound together?"

Mike: "Exactly. You do what you can with what you have with you. It just wasn't very effective."

Phil: "It seems you were more concerned about his wounds and bleeding than you were about making your extraction time, at least in those moments. I would think he had to be leaking all over the place."

Mike: "I got it stopped pretty good. You do what you can with what you've got. That place I stopped at was pretty wet. I dug down and made like a mud pie. I put that on him and then wrapped around it. That was actually one of the most effective dressings. We were taught that in survival training. I did everything I was trained, everything morally and compassionately I could think of to do I did trying to help him."

Phil: "You thought he was still with you for most of this ordeal?"

Mike: "I know he was for at least 90 percent; I was checking about once each hour. And then the more I got close to, closer to the border, the more I would, I was concentrating on getting there more than anything else. There's nothing more I could have done to save him."

Phil: "When they found you, how close were you to the extraction LZ?"

Mike: "I don't know. I'd guess within, I'm going to say, probably within a half mile. It happened really fast. I heard the chopper; I popped the green smoke, and they came right in."

Phil: "Yeah, so they were looking for you. They know this is your only hope. Just look at the way he dove in. He might have been low on fuel. You might have been a little on the late side of the pickup time. Once he saw your smoke, they just dove right in. That's not characteristic. Part of what that says to me is he'd probably been on station for some time looking for you.

"He sees the smoke—'Holy bleep, there's the smoke. Let's go get them.'

"Those guys had to be excited to have found you. I can see them jumping up and down in their seats. Plus, this was the third and final attempt. Would they have come back the next day?"

Mike: "I don't think so. We were told, 'You have three attempts to make it out. If you're not there on the third attempt, we are going to assume you are captured or dead.'

Phil: "And what if you were there and they weren't or didn't see your smoke, and now you have night coming, what do you do? Are there enemy forces patrolling?"

Mike: "Jonathan was still on my back. If I rolled him off, I'd have realized he had died. I'd put him someplace under a tree or a bush and mark it and continue on. Crawling. I would have more than likely run across a patrol. Sooner or later, most likely a North Vietnamese patrol."

Phil: "But you were in South Vietnam."

Mike: "Yes, and this area very close to Laos was not an area we heavily patrolled. Our bases were all further west. This was no-man's land with more patrols from the North than our guys. I would have covered him up and marked his location in such a way that I could find him. I'd have kept going west, fifty/fifty chance friendly or foe. But I probably would have bled out within twenty-four hours. Yeah, this leg was all messed up. I'd have probably bled out; it was really bad."

Phil: "If that had happened. If you had marked the location of Jonathan's body and then been rescued, would they have allowed you or would they have sent a patrol out to go looking for him?"

Mike: "I don't know. I don't think so. I'd have gone back anyway. It was Jonathan. Marines bring back our dead brothers."

Phil: "Okay, the guys that fixed your leg for you did a really good job."

Mike: "The navy corpsman, I mean, they're very good people. The doc that helped me was good."

Phil: "And maybe later the physical therapy folks you worked with helped with your recovery too? But what was it, was it the tendons that needed to be repaired?"

Mike: "I had shrapnel go in three or four places. Some went through and came out on the other side. In my surgeries, they were digging stuff out. Not a lot of stuff. There was two pieces, I think, that they pulled out. But what had gone through took ligaments, vessels, everything with it."

Phil: "Are you saying you didn't really have much mobility at all?"

Mike: "I had no feeling or mobility on my lower leg."

Phil: "You could move up through the thigh?"

Mike: "I could, but below the knee, it just wasn't functional. There was nothing. All the nerves and everything were traumatized to the foot. My boot was on. It was laced up. I didn't have occasion to take it off."

Phil: "I was in a bad car accident as a teenager, broke my leg in the collision but felt no pain because of shock. Did you have pain?"

Mike: "I knew I was wounded. I knew I was wounded badly. But it did not hurt to where I'm groaning or moaning. It was like a dull ache until I saw Katye coming down. I guess my adrenaline started to wear off a little bit."

Phil: "Did you take any morphine for the pain?"

Mike: "No, there wasn't any left. I used all we had on Jonathan. The morphine syrettes were sort of like a small tube of airplane glue with a needle on the end. They were available to anyone going into the field. You carried them in your vest if you wanted. We always carried them. We each had two. I used my two on Jonathan at the booby trap. I used his two, the first about three hours in when he started groaning, the second sometime later."

Phil: "And both you guys were carrying bandages. I mean you used everything you carried in terms of your medical gear."

Mike: "Oh yeah, I used everything, plus my sleeves, plus dirt, you know, mud, everything I had at my disposal, trying to help him. For me, it was a matter of a tourniquet above my knee with my belt. Then I put him back on my back and off we went."

Phil: "I'm wondering about these stories. They sound like rumors, you know, of people being killed and eviscerated and all this stuff. Were those stories scuttlebutt, or was that actually...?"

Mike: "They are accurate. Usually, a Marine or an army scout, the guy had gotten captured. They would be strung up on a fence, stripped, disemboweled while they are still alive. The village pigs would be allowed to feed on them. Think about that. These poor souls are carved open, watching as the starving pigs come running. They would, after they died, cut off genitals and shove them down their throat."

Phil: "I had heard that was common in Vietnam."

Mike: "They were, I'm not going to say masters, but at cruel torture, they were very good. Barbaric torture, they were very good. They would behead guys. They would torture to make us scream. To have your friends hear you screaming.

"So then you're going to try to come to the screamer's rescue and save them. And they'd have a trap set up. Don't go unless you have a whole group of people to go with you because that is what they are trying to do. To sucker you in.

"Certain snipers on their side would try to wound, not kill, us. They want you hurt and even better hurt so you are crying out for help so they can pick off your buddies when they come in to rescue you. The horrors of war are, you know, just too hard, too barbaric to remember.

"And the villages. You know about half at least of the villagers are NVA supporters. If you dug around enough, you'd find ammo, munitions, food for the enemy. All that stuff. We never could know which ones are giving you a smile as you walk by when, after dark, they will be out there looking to help kill you.

"This colonel sent in the little kids into our camps with grenades strapped around them. Killing kids to get us."

Phil: "So you're saying kids would be used to get onto our bases? They'd come around looking for candy bars or whatever?"

Mike: "Yeah, that's one of the things most guys would carry. Candy, you know. These guys were telling them how they could go about doing that. I mean, the kids didn't know. They were so young. They didn't understand if you pull this, you're going to blow yourself up. They don't understand that. They were trained in such a way. I can't even imagine how…that once you're around American soldiers, you've got to pull this little ring. And it happened, to my knowledge, at least a dozen times. When the opportunity came up to go hunt this guy, I raised my hand."

Phil: "You guys had heard that this was going on?"

Mike: "Oh, it was. It was. It was bad. It was making it bad on the innocent people, the Vietnamese innocent people because they couldn't get away."

Phil: "These stories of attacks at your base or adjoining camps or neighboring camps. Was this like one soldier telling another soldier? One Marine telling another Marine?"

Mike: "There were a lot of Associated Press photographers and writers that would accompany our guys at the base. They were not allowed to go out on what we called hunter/killer patrols. They weren't allowed."

Phil: "Were they billeted (do they live) somewhere near you guys?"

Mike: "They were billeted right with us. They would go around and talk to the soldiers, the Marines, and report what they heard."

Phil: "Were the officers billeted directly with you?"

Mike: "No. No, they had their own private area in one part of the camp. Near the center of the camp. Whenever possible, they were billeted underground."

Phil: "Were you guys too?"

Mike: "No, not unless we had the time to dig our own. I was never billeted underground."

Phil: "Even in the rain?"

Mike: "Yeah, even in the rain."

Phil: "How many at your camp?"

Mike: "Maybe 500. Somewhere around 350 were combat grunts carrying rifles, the rest support."

Phil: "Were you on sentry duty in addition to your assignments?"

Mike: "I never had to do sentry duty. I volunteered for it a few times when I heard there could be the possibility of an attack. I'd rather be out there on the line shooting at somebody than in my billet listening to them coming. I could defend myself on the line, so I volunteered."

Phil: "And what are you guys eating in the field at the camp?"

Mike: "Depends on where we were. Anything from K rats and C rats to hot cooked meals. Some camps have hot food, some camps not. The big camp had hot food most of the time. The outside camps would get hot food flown in once or twice a week. They'd bring it in by air when we weren't under attack. If we were, we'd go to C rats or K rats. The C rats, in my opinion, weren't that bad."

Phil: "Where was the ammo dump in the camp?"

Mike: "It was usually buried underground as close to the middle of the camp as possible."

Phil: "Radios?"

Mike: "Not many radios. Some at the command center. Mainly for calling in reports and requesting support. We had no radios when we went out."

Phil: "Where were the helicopters?"

Mike: "They were south of us at a bigger, safer base where there was less likelihood of an attack. We had a pickup LZ at our camp that they used.

"Setting up a camp, the Seabees would come in with their bull-dozers. Those guys were brave. If it was going to be a big camp, they would create an open strip all around the perimeter. They would create it around the entire camp. We called it a kill zone. They would go out there with their dozers and mow down the jungle. They were smart. They would build metal plate protection around the inside of the tractor. If they got shot at, small arms fire, they couldn't hit them. For the bulldozers, they'd just raise the blade up. If they saw where the fire was coming from, they'd raise the blade and go straight for it. They were all armed, of course, and most of them, when they were operating equipment, would have one or two infantry troops with them. They earned their pay. That's how close the NVA were. They were watching all the time and when they wanted taking the random shot.

"The kill zone is out against the jungle. They would cut it in at least a couple hundred yards minimum, then you'd have your concertina wire. That's the big silver rolls of razor wire like three feet high, rolls on rolls. We'd take empty cans, hang them up on the wire, and put rocks in them. That way those cans would make noise if someone was moving the wire or through the wire. That helped us know they were coming. They usually would come at night.

"If we had the time and the resources, we would run blue gas out there that could be detonated. Blue gas burns close to the ground when we set it off. We dug these trenches and rigged tubing to allow this heavy blue gas to flow into the trenches when we thought or knew we heard them. A little fire in a trench is a great deterrent. And we had claymores. They are explosive mines. They would be up against our protection, right in front of you. Just a little way out from our sentries beyond the concertina wire."

Phil: "So while they were fighting to get through, you'd blow off the claymores?"

Mike: "Yeah, that claymore was a deadly, wonderful invention. They would be set off by trip wire, or the ones closer in we could detonate electronically. They are rectangular and have a half moon shape with two or two hundred fifty pellets, like double aught shotgun pellets with a C-4 charge behind it. When a claymore goes off, the pellets just spray out. It's a beautiful thing. Pretty effective.

"We had to learn the hard way. Sometimes, their sentries would come sneaking in and turn the claymores around. Claymores fresh out of the bag are green on both sides. So we got smart and started painting the back side, the side facing us or the dirt, white. It took a few people killed to figure that out.

"The purpose of painting the backs white was so we could quickly check to see if they were facing the right direction. When the attack would come, we'd go and set one off. Thing is, if they had turned it around we'd be setting it off against ourselves.

"So we learned, and we painted the back sides white. Then we could go out and check our claymores, and if they showed white, they had to be turned around.

"It's not surprising that people at war figure out how to use everything in the field against the other guy. The Vietnamese people lived in the field. They were conniving. They were smart. We had to learn the hard way. When we first got there, we weren't very good at jungle warfare. A lot of good Americans lost their lives just because of improper training. Punji sticks, booby traps, and all this stuff. All low tech, nothing fancy about them, but effective, very effective.

"The Mel Gibson movie *We Were Soldiers* has Sam Elliot playing Sergeant Major Basil Plumley. Sergeant Majors are the senior enlisted man in the outfit, and if it's an infantry unit, those guys are battle tested and tough as nails. This soldier was a genuine warrior. He had served among heroes. He was a hero. I met the real guy. He went by John. The movie was extremely accurate, which I would expect because of Colonel Moore and Joe Galloway. The book is fantastic, even better.

"The John I met was the manager of a limo company in San Diego. I met him just a few years back while working for an insurance company some forty odd years after the war. I went in to do my normal inspections and everything. You know, I got a feeling. My sixth sense went on alert. There was something about the guy. I could just tell from the way he carried himself, the way he spoke. He had that military bearing about him.

"When we got done with our business, I said, 'Okay, what branch?'

"He said, 'Army.'

"I don't know why, but I held back my normal cocky Marine comeback. I'd often say with some attitude to the normal army vet, 'I'm sorry.' Then we would stand there and banter for a bit. Many times, these random conversations would take fifteen, twenty minutes. And with some guys, thirty seconds or less. With John, I just felt a sense of brotherhood. Suddenly, we were communicating without even talking."

"He says, 'Yeah, 101st Airborne and 7th Cavalry.'

"I asked him, 'Were you with Hal Moore?'

"He says, 'Yeah, I was there. Sam Elliot did a very good job portraying me.'

"Now, I've got tears coming down my cheeks. So we talked some more. And then, I ask, 'Okay, I've got one question. Forget the war. Forget everything else. What happened to you afterward?' I'm thinking of the issues that I'm going through.

"He says, 'It was ugly. I lost my wife. I lost my kids. I couldn't hold a job. For five years, I buried myself in a bottle of Jack Daniel's.'

"Then a big smile came to his face. 'One day, I went back to my hometown, and I went back to the church that I'd been raised in. At the end of the service, the pastor walks out with me. He's a true country pastor. He says, "John, it's time you get your head out of your ass." See, country.'

"He says, 'I started reading the Bible. I started leaning on the Lord. I tried taking one step and then another. I got my wife back. I got my kids back. I got a good job.' John says, 'I needed hope. My faith gave me hope.'

"That was one of the most meaningful conversations I've ever had."

Phil: "Something has helped you get through your experiences."

Mike: "Yes, the Lord. That line I opened back in the jungle; it still is."

Phil: "Would you say that most scout/snipers would feel comfortable at five hundred yards they're going to get the intended target?"

Mike: "If we didn't, we weren't a sniper. We were trained out to a thousand yards. One shot, one kill."

Phil: "I know you are a natural shot, but you had to practice to keep that skill high. You had to have practiced regularly?"

Mike: "I tried to shoot every few days, even when in camp. I wanted to keep my feel for my rifle very high. One with the rifle.

"I had to go to the command for permission and then would shoot off eight to ten rounds at targets out on one side of our camp. They didn't want us spooking the locals. The command sergeant would let the guys on guard duty know it was us so they wouldn't panic either. I'd pick out some object a fair distance out and do all my adjustments for elevation, distance, wind, and angle and take a shot. And adjust from there. Always working on one shot, one kill."

Phil: "Did we have guard dogs?"

Mike: "I heard there were dogs with our troops in Vietnam, but I never saw one."

Phil: "Did you find it difficult to shoot people, or did you feel like the training had prepared you?"

Mike: "Prepared. But again, there is a real difference between where you are behind a wire or out hunting the enemy with a couple of platoons of your buddies. In those battles, people are running at you and trying to shoot and kill you as they come. When you are shooting back, there's a good distance between you and them. When your aim is on and you hit a man coming at you, you aren't close enough to see what happens to him. If you are, you are in big trouble because grunts have artillery and close air support, fixed wing, helicopter, air force, other grunts, everything to call in when they get in too close. So they don't get that close very often.

"Most firefights, the enemy would come at us. They would engage our guys that were out in the field. They knew the terrain better than we did. It was rare for us to catch them in the open and have a chance to start in on them. Sometimes, with intel, it could happen, but it was rare. When our grunts are attacked, they attack harder. The enemy troops engaging go down. The NVA, off the line, often vanish. They knew the jungle and had lots of underground tunnels. They were here shooting at us one minute, then a moment later they aren't even here. There was quite a bit of that.

"Snipers are trained to watch your target. Carlos told us, 'You've got to watch that guy through your scope to validate the kill. And sometimes, you're going to see a head explode. You've got to get used to it. Put this in your mind: every time you are successful, you are saving human lives. Every time.' That pretty much got me through. Then too, when you get back from a little outing, if at all possible, you get a pint of Jack."

Only Move When Their Back Is to You—I Never Missed

Mike: "The South Vietnamese forces were good fighters. The ones I enjoyed the most were a couple of times when I was in Laos, I had Laotian guides. Little, very short, like, four-foot-six guy wearing only a loincloth, barefooted, more accurate with a bow and arrow at a hundred yards than most Marines with an M14. Couldn't speak a word of English. Knew hand signals. They were wonderful people. They hated the communists. They lived off the land. True, true natives. They were growing rice in the fields. Killing animals in the wild. Doing whatever they needed to do to survive. They were badly persecuted by the North Vietnamese. Every time I had the opportunity to go into Laos, I would try, if possible, to meet some of these people. It didn't happen very often, but when it did, it was a pleasure.

"The Hmong guide would take me to a target location. They knew the country like the back of your hand. I would show them on my map where I wanted to go. He'd just motion with his hand, as if he had a back pocket, telling me to put the map away. They eat raw fish. He knew the stuff out of the ground you could eat, stuff out of the ground you couldn't eat. I learned a lot from him."

Phil: "Who did you report to?"

Mike: "Scout/sniper teams were attached to infantry battalions. T/O (table of operations) was five teams. We were never at T/O. We had three teams all working different assignments, different areas, supporting different units. I had a sergeant and a lieutenant that I talked to. The sergeant was more a messenger. The lieutenant, whenever we had a mission come up, would give me the information.

"On each mission, I had the prerogative. It was always mine. I would let them know that I would take an assignment. I would begin preparing because certain things needed to take place. Number one, diet. Number two, terrain. We planned the way in, the way out, what maps to prepare, which maps to carry. I often needed at least a week. Sometimes, a bit more.

"My last mission, we were almost two weeks preparing. They didn't know with true certainty which weekend this colonel would be given the liberty he had coming. They said he was going to the mansion. It was the out of country resort the NVA officers frequented. I was eating that food longer than I really wanted."

Phil: "Tell us about the food."

Mike: "You basically eat what the Vietnamese or the Laotian people in the region you will be operating in eat. It constitutes of bugs, raw fish, rice, vegetables, roots, and so forth. And nothing to drink but water. The local water had a different taste to it than what we drank in our camps. Most of ours was bottled and brought in or in a big water buffalo next to the mess area. So we had to get water from the area we are going to. They would give me the pills to purify it, so it didn't give me dysentery or something like that. Yeah, and no booze. No liquor of any kind because it has an odor. A distinct odor. Water in streams has to travel about one hundred feet over rocks and sand to become good drinking water. The water plus foods—bugs, fish, rice, roots, vegetables, meat, fish, mostly fish."

Phil: "I would imagine the local fish was pretty good."

Mike: "Not really. It was so, so bitterly salty."

Phil: "What about the insects, how was that? How do you put them in your mouth?"

Mike: "Fried crickets, grasshoppers, whatever, they would fry them up. Very high protein. Bugs are naturally crunchy in the mouth. Bugs in Vietnam were big. At first, hard to put in your mouth, hard to eat, but you get used to it. It's one of the reasons I don't partake of much Asian food today."

Phil: "What's a breakfast?"

Mike: "All the things. Most meals are pretty much the same. They only eat twice a day and not near as much as we do. They are a very poor, very thin, very fit people."

Phil: "Did they have eggs?"

Mike: "Chicken eggs were sometimes available but very rare. You don't see too many chickens in the villages. The ones that were there were scrawny."

Phil: "Where did you get this food?"

Mike: "I'd put in the request. They'd have it for me at the mess hall. But I wouldn't eat it in the mess hall. I started to one time, the odor of it, this one guy sitting nearby says, 'Yuck! Dude, that stinks.' So I'd picked it up and ate it back at my own place."

Phil: "Where was your place?"

Mike: "It was a dugout hole with a two-person tent but usually just me. You know, two shelter halves. I had a cot to keep my bag up off the dirt. Me and my gear. I'd sleep with my weapon under the cot, my knife under my pillow. I'd walk over to the mess hall, pick up my food, go back there and eat it. Sometimes, I had a little stove, and I'd fire it up. Some of what they ate was cooked over an open fire. We were trying to duplicate what they do. They used a sauce. I'll call it soy sauce, but it wasn't soy sauce. It was a concoction of whatever spices they put in everything. Very, very strong ginger root. Overwhelming. It was hard to eat. The first couple of times I tried eating a meal through with that sauce, I almost threw up. It made you gag. It had its own unique set of flavors and combinations. Lemongrass too. Chilies, mint, cilantro, and dill.

"I stayed to myself. Most snipers do. The next guy over was more than twenty yards away. We were spaced out I think I told you for the mortars. If you got around grunts, they'd want to know what we were doing. I didn't want to talk about it. None of their business, and they asked too many questions. Besides, our assignments often were secret, another reason I didn't want to tell anyone anything.

"We had to be careful when we went into a village. Guys would see hungry people and try to give out food, but our food would give them dysentery real quick. We had to learn to tell them to eat just a little bit.

"In combat situations, you don't always have time to put your rifle in your shoulder and aim. So you had to develop really good hand-eye coordination to be able to aim and shoot from the hip.

"My brother and I, as kids, used to go out to the dump. We would take wine bottles and throw them up in the air, then snap shoot from the hip. Growing up and shooting doves out of the back of my dad's moving pickup truck. All of these shooting skills helped prepare me more than any of the training in the Marine Corps.

"You've got to give them credit. They pulled Carlos in from the field with over ninety confirmed kills with truly more like very close to three hundred because of the way kills were confirmed. You had to have a witness of the kill, and he liked being alone. Or if no witness, bring back to camp a body part. Unless the target is entirely alone, which is not very likely, going to retrieve some part is way too risky. And a really gross idea to begin with. Who wants to walk back with a bloody body part? Or get caught trying to retrieve one or carrying one out? I never did that.

"We worked at being one with the rifle. In time, shooting at targets a good distance out there day after day, we did improve and then the next day improve some more. Each time we worked a hunt, we were constantly scanning for elevation, distance, wind, and using our experience and training, picking aiming points and making sight adjustments to bring the one shot, one kill mantra to reality."

Phil: "Did you have shooting contests and competitions?"

Mike: "Oh yeah, back at the school, and they were fun. They'd start out at one hundred yards and then move further out. Some of the good ones—Carlos would set up a target at one thousand yards and give us a scenario. Once he put us on a little knoll with the target downhill to teach us. He says, 'If you're shooting downhill, your bullet's going to rise. You may think you need to compensate a foot or so, but you don't. Your bullet is going downhill. It's going to pick up velocity. Now shooting uphill, just the opposite.'

"Toward the end of scout/sniper school, we were given a course to test our skills. You have a target to hit. Your assignment is to get within one hundred yards of the target undetected and make the shot. You are four hundred yards or more away when you start. Instructors are in the field as observers, and sentries are moving about in the area you are trying to traverse. There are more spotters as you get closer in. They gave us three chances. Most people didn't make it on their first try. Took me two. If you didn't pass, you could start the school all over from the beginning or go back to your former unit. I never saw anyone go back.

"Getting caught wasn't the camouflage. It was the way you moved. You only moved when their back was to you. That's one thing Carlos pounded into us. You never move when somebody is facing you. Their eye might catch something. Even if you think your movement might be seen as a limb waving in the breeze. That motion could just look off, not right. Don't move.

"They didn't have end covers for the scope back then. At least we didn't. We went out on our own and got a bicycle tube at the PX [post exchange; base retail store] and cut it so we could stretch it over the scope. The black rubber covers the glass. Covered, sunlight won't bounce off and create a glare or a flash. That's what gave a lot of people away—the sun. If possible, always have the sun at your back."

Phil: "Did you miss?"

Mike: "I never missed. Period, end of story. I never missed. Sometimes I didn't hit exactly where I wanted to hit, but every shot I took was always a fatal shot. Each time the guy just crumpled. There's no fallback. There's no lurch like you see in the movies. They just crumpled. Everything stops. All motor skills stop. Life ceases to exist. They drop. Boom.

"The person that's being shot never hears the rifle because the bullet is supersonic. They aren't there to hear it when the sound arrives. They never know it's coming. They're just instantly gone. Boom. Gone.

"It's like when my dad and I were out shooting targets at four hundred yards in a dry creek bed. When I'm marking targets for him, I'm standing off to the side but within maybe fifteen feet of the target. When he took a shot, I'd hear the bullet hitting the paper before hearing the rifle discharge. It'd be maybe a fraction of a second or whatever later. You'd hear the paper. Sort of splat. Then you'd hear the report of the rifle. Crack.

"Another of our favorite contests was to, on the way back from a day out with ranchers, Dad and I, we'd have a shooting contest. We'd both be ready for jackrabbits. We'd shoot at them out the pickup window. Nothing under four hundred yards. He'd have the first one, or sometimes it would be me. We just skipped back and forth. He was hard to beat.

"You've got to watch that you don't shoot out the rearview mirror. It can just shatter. I did it once. He'd pull over and stop. I'm bringing my rifle up to rest on the open door as I stepped out with his stop. I just got too quick this time, too close. Maybe I didn't hit the mirror, but I probably did. Or the concussion of a very close round caused it, but it just shattered. My dad wasn't happy about that. I ended up paying for the mirror.

"The last deer I killed...I mean, the last two deer I killed. We were coming home from Colorado. We were just ahead of a snowstorm. We'd been hunting there, hadn't had any luck at all. Both of our rifles are in the cab on the front seat of the pickup next to us. A buck and a doe jumped across the road and headed up the side of this mountain. He pulls over. We don't see any cars. I bail out and lean over the hood of the truck. I dropped the buck. He was going to get the doe. He was on her. My round got there first. I dropped the doe before he fired. Both of them are down about one hundred yards up there.

"Dad said, 'Okay, smart-ass. You beat me to it. Looks like you get to go up there and get them.'

"And it's fitting as my last two deer killed, they were both running shots. My dad trained me if a deer is running away, you don't want to hit him in the rear quarter. Butt shots—not good. The deer's head, as he runs, will come up and go down, come up and go down in a rhythm. You time it so you shoot when the deer's head is down. By the time the bullet gets there, the head will be up. When the buck went down, the doe turned and veered in a new direction. Now, she was running parallel to me. I just aimed at her nose. The bullet hit her in the heart. Those are things I was taught out with my dad as a kid. Those lessons were invaluable later when I was out hunting as a Marine.

"If you have an enemy soldier running, you start making the same kind of adjustments in addition to factoring in for distance, elevation, and wind. If he's within, say, one hundred yards, just a lead of a couple of inches ahead. If it's three, four, or five hundred, each one a bit more lead up to as much as a head length lead. We were always making those kind of leading shots and letting the guy run into the bullet.

"In training, we were moving across a field with targets out three hundred yards or so, and the targets were moving away from us. We were expected to hit in at least the nine ring. That meant either in the bullseye or the first ring out from in the bullseye. Carlos says, 'You've got black targets with white rings moving away from you. Aim for the leading edge of the black and let the bullet drift to the bullseye.' We picked reference points like that. Carlos helped us get better and better,

"You know when a bullet leaves a rifle, it's going to rise a little bit as it accelerates and from there, it will begin to drop a little. We would zero our scope to four hundred yards. At four hundred yards, the bullet is on the same plane. At three hundred, it will be a little high of the aiming point. Five hundred, a bit low of the aiming point. If we had a six hundred-yard shot, we aim above the head a few inches, and you're going to be fine.

"Because the final assignment, we had set up our hide nearly seven hundred yards out, I was aiming a fair bit above the top of his head.

All of our assignments, all of our training, all we ever did was head shots. I knew I was going to get him somewhere between forehead and neck. That's a lot of latitude as long as vertical alignment is on."

Phil: "Still, at this distance, hitting a target that's a bit smaller than a basketball is an amazing shot. Even for a gifted Marine scout/sniper."

Mike: "We got there early enough that we were watching everything toward where he would likely be so we could make the correct adjustments. But wind was not a factor. We watched the leaves near the target, saw the flags were limp, watched as the dust would swirl and settle to the ground coming off the turning wheels of the trucks. The puffs of dust would bellow out from the wheel wells and just settle. No drift. We checked everything. We didn't have to worry about windage.

"You had to shoot to the point where you knew what the rifle was going to do. What the bullet was going to do. My dad taught me marksmanship. Carlos taught me how to prepare, how to be patient, and how to survive. I don't think Marine boot camp did anything for my rifle skills.

"Carlos helped me get my head in the right place to live with what we were doing. Even now, it's still hard. I'm still learning how to cope. I do find at this stage of my life, I lean more on the Lord each day."

WALKING BACK—HE'S READY

Phil: "Do you know when scout/sniper school originated?"

Mike: "A friend of mine served in Korea. The sniper school didn't exist during Korea. If you were a good shot, they just gave you a scope for your rifle and said, 'Go do it.' Vietnam was the first theater that incorporated the Marine Corps scout/sniper school to formalize training and preparation. When the captain, the company commander, at boot camp told us about the school and then said 'Hathcock,' and we'd heard about his tales and all this stuff, I say, 'Yeah, that sounds good. When do I leave?' He says, 'About forty-eight hours after graduation.'"

Phil: "So you were too young to have any fear?"

Mike: "Yeah, and full of piss and vinegar being brainwashed by the Marine Corps that we're the best. We're the best. We're the invincible ones. We're better than the army. They actually did acknowledge that at the time. The Green Berets, the Navy SEALS. They say to you that a basic Marine is as qualified as a Green Beret or a Navy SEAL. Now, they may have a little more technical expertise in certain areas and a few more muscles. They claim to have more brains too. But we, as to general training, are as good."

Phil: "What was the physical aspect of scout/sniper school? Were they still running you and PTing you like crazy?"

Mike: "Oh yeah. I mean, the Marine Corps had the doctrine that combat was not as tough as training. That doctrine saved a lot of lives. That's why most of our exercises were done with live ammo."

Phil: "I was always impressed with our entire group of leaders at OCS. All of those officers and NCOs were very fit, very in-shape, very squared-away Marines."

Mike: "Yes, and all our DIs [drill instructors] could run you into the dirt. When we did PT, they were right there doing it with us and not showing a sweat. They were on us all the time and seemed to love what they were doing. I only had that one prima donna, Sergeant Lindsey.

"After boot camp, I got one weekend leave, and then I was on a train to Camp Lejeune in North Carolina. Three-day cross-country trip. I slept most of the time. They said you can wear your civilian clothes on the train. You won't get your uniforms messed up or wrinkled. I thought about this later. There were protests and demonstrations going on in those years. I think they said wear civvies because of that."

Phil: "So now it was different. Now you are going to a school as a Marine. You are wearing the uniform."

Mike: "Yeah, once you are allowed to blouse your pants. It's a tradition. It doesn't happen until the final week of boot camp. Now, you're a Marine. You're one of us. (Marines wear their utility trousers cuffed under and held by springs bloused to their boot tops. Recruits do not.) We loved looking like we knew how to wear the uniform.

"Laos was considered enemy country even though off limits. We were given assignments. The word 'target' was never used. They didn't want us talking, if we were not on base, about this person or that person. We would just say we had an assignment. We were not allowed to say where because 90 percent of our stuff was in Laos, which we weren't supposed to be in."

Phil: "The first time you go out, are you by yourself, or do they send you with somebody?"

Mike: "I got paired up with a veteran scout/sniper. We both had weapons. His task on this assignment was basically to see if I was ready. After that, I would ask to go by myself, which I preferred. I mean, Carlos kind of beat it into us, "Don't take a spotter with you. He's going to get killed.' He says, 'More than 75 percent of my times out, I was alone.' I tried going alone as much as possible. It ended up that for me something close to half the time, they let me go alone."

Phil: "More about your rifle. You were using an M1A1?

Mike: "Well, I had actually two. Both are precision weapons. You had your choice of the M1A1 or a Remington 700. They're both 7.62 mm rounds. The Remington 700 is bolt action. The magazine held five rounds."

Phil: "Clip?"

Mike: "There's no clip in it. Open the barrel, load rounds by pushing them down into the magazine. It's built in. Bolt action.

"The M1A1 Super Match was a Springfield M14 with a chrome-lined Douglas barrel, and the locking bolt that chambers the round has four lugs instead of two for better seating and extraction. It also had a slightly longer barrel. Yeah, chromoly, they call it. The inside of the barrel is chromed. Very much more accurate."

Phil: "What kind of ammunition are you using? Just standard?"

Mike: "No, they would give us what they called Super Match ammunition. We had a choice: hollow point or solid point. Usually 180-grain bullets. That's the weight of the bullet. They varied from 165 to 190 grain. For whatever reason, the ballistics of the M14 liked the 180 grain.

"My six-millimeter rifle I had as a kid, it liked 105-grain rounds. I mean, I could sit there and do targets—hollow points, pointed points, and round nose. The round nose gives me a better group every time. That's what I would use, and all my six millimeters were hand loaded by my mom.

"My mom was the official bullet maker in our family. She had a manual scale she used from the vet lab. She loaded powder by the grain and exact amounts grain by grain until perfect. We had the best loads you could get. When we were away on calls or out hunting, she had time to load for me and my dad. I saw him do things with his rifle—I'd tell stories, and people would just shake their heads."

Phil: "Why did you have only nine kills?"

Mike: "I had more than nine, just nine confirmed kills. Sometimes you'd go out, and your target wouldn't be there. I probably had twenty to twenty-five assignments. But if the assignment wasn't there, we were strictly instructed, if no target, don't pull your trigger. Because if we did, they would know we are hunting that area. They will move.

"When I remember all the briefings, all the preparation, and stuff, yes, I have nine confirmed kills. I think in total, it was about sixteen, but I couldn't confirm the others.

"Besides, part of the role is reconnaissance. That's a scout/sniper's second line of duty: advanced reconnaissance. Many of my missions were to go out and take notes of what we saw. On those assignments, we were only to use force if force was being used on us."

Phil: "They would assign you to go into an area of known enemy activity. To hide out there in a place where you can see the movements on roads or trails. To stay there for two, three days before you sneak back?"

Mike: "Exactly. That was probably the majority of my assignments. Some of those were Vietnam, and some of those might have been Laos. There was a lot of troop and weapon movement on the border, coming down the trail. The NVA were coming from the north in waves, thousands and thousands of troops on the move, coming to do combat; we could help our guys get an idea of the specifics of the movement. Locations, numbers. Help assess the threat. How many, how armed, anything that would help us know what they were up to. Which of our camps were they heading to. Many times what we learned and passed up the chain helped our guys set up defenses or prepare for attacks. The information we gathered saved lives.

"My camp was east of Dong Ha, way up north close to the DMZ [the demilitarized zone] and the border with North Vietnam. It was inland from the coast a good ways to the east, not that far from Laos. I'd say I was out on assignments about two-thirds of the time. After an assignment, I'd have two or three days off. Just to decompress. Maybe catch some sleep. Drink my pint or whatever. Jack Daniel's helped me decompress.

"I would report on each assignment. We didn't do handwritten reports. It was all verbal. Some poor clerk had to do the transcribing. In addition to preparing my body by eating their food, I'd prepare by studying. I'd memorize what the target looks like, what his actions are. I'd memorize details."

Phil: "How many times did your command let you go alone?"

Mike: "Not many, maybe half. It depended on the target. If I was going into an area where it was what they termed a 'target-rich environment'—you know, lots of enemy—I had to have a spotter. If I was going to an area that was remote, then I didn't. We were very proficient at map reading, no GPS back then. All I had was my compass, a flashlight, and a map. I could look at the stars and pretty much tell where I was. When I left the base, I would look up and find the brightest star I could. That's the way I kind of kept my bearings.

"You've got to plan and play out the mission in your mind ahead of time. You know how far. You have the topical maps. Sometimes you have flyover imagery, not often, but sometimes. So you could literally do that mission in your head before you went off. It was a big help. When I got out there, there was no 'What do I do now?' We made sure we were as prepared as we could be. You know, Marines. Hoorah."

Phil: "The final mission, you hit a trip wire. Did that happen before?"

Mike: "On two or three occasions, I spotted the trip wire and stepped over it or went around it. Those were times I was walking. This time, the fear of the dogs or the other guys coming after us had us running.

"We got to where we could spot them. Usually, it's because the brush is not laying just right. If the sun happens to be shining on it, you can sometimes get a little glimmer off the wire. Sometimes you can spot the device they are using to hold the grenade. They often strapped the tubes to a tree. What many people don't realize is that the device is set up to fling the grenade out in front of your path. Where you will be, not where you are when you trip it. They were very smart that way. Very smart."

Phil: "Was your camp being assaulted?"

Mike: "It got attacked a couple of times. We had the two- to three-hundred-yard open area, killing field, that the Seabees had cut out. We put wire, we put blue gas, we put claymores. You name it, it went out there. Toward the end of the war, that's one of the reasons the major attacks on our camps pretty much subsided. We had built up the defenses around these bases so that the NVA were going to have too many losses to attack. When it was during construction, they knew all of our defenses weren't there, weren't set up yet. During construction, there were more attacks."

Phil: "Your assignments. Did you walk, jeep, truck, chopper?"

Mike: "Over twenty miles, we were flown out. Under five miles, we would often hump. It just depended on the circumstances, what the timeframe was. What is the terrain? What distance will we have to cover at night to get into position? There were so many variables."

Phil: "About half the time, you walked your way back?"

Mike: "Yes, and if we were walking back in, we had somewhat of an idea of where our friendly patrols would be. Where our guys might be planning to be over the next few days. We didn't want to get shot at by our own guys coming back. We would have words, passwords. There's a lot of words that some languages can't say. Like the Japanese. The letter *r* is not in their language. So we had certain code words so our sentries would know. And our patrols were told you might be encountering a returning Marine coming back. But the patrols were still being careful too.

"The NVA, occasionally, would pull the clothes off a dead Marine and put them on. But when they tried that, the lack of talking was a dead giveaway. Plus, the size. Most Marines are nearly a foot taller with a broader body structure than any Vietnamese. Some, like Sgt. Dibble, two feet taller. Often, it wasn't hard to know that wasn't a Marine in a Marine uniform. It wasn't that hard. You'd give those guys a chance up to about twenty-five yards, and if they wouldn't verbally respond to us, they were shot. That simple.

"You never knew when you walked through a village. Are they friendly? You never knew if they had a cache of weapons, a cache of explosives. The NVA soldiers would torture the Vietnamese people in the south, their own people, to keep them submissive to them."

Phil: "After you came home, how did you adjust to being away from that intensity?"

Mike: "Most of my adjustment was done in the hospital. At Balboa. After the surgery while rehabbing my leg. I got to talk. We didn't have psychiatrists and all this stuff, but you got to talk to the other wounded soldiers. You got to talk to the nurses that had seen a lot of wounded Marines. Those ladies would sit down and talk to you for hours. Some of them would come in on their own, even when they aren't on duty. They would just sit down and talk. I got most of my anxieties talked out."

Phil: "When did you see your dad after getting out?"

Mike: "It was probably six months after. I went down to go out dove hunting with my dad. I was grappling with if I ever wanted to shoot another weapon. After what I had been doing, I just wasn't sure. I had to work through it in my mind. I had a gunnery sergeant I met one time; I never knew his name. We were talking, and he says, 'What you did you were trained for. You were ordered to do it, and you had God's blessing. Don't ever let anyone ever take that away from you. Every time you were successful, you saved lives.' And Carlos had said the same thing."

Phil: "Some people would see you as an assassin."

Mike: "Yes and saving our guys' or our friends' lives each and every time."

Phil: "This Marine Corps time we have talked about, your ordeal that you have lived through must be a huge part your life experience."

Mike: "Oh yeah, it's that. Number one, it showed me how far I could push myself. A lot of people would have shot themselves up with morphine. Sat there in a daze until they got caught. And then we'd be dead. Death would not have been pleasant. Marines were not dealt with very pleasantly by the North Vietnamese.

"It taught me how to survive. It taught me work ethic, even though I pretty much had that. But mission, mission, mission. One of the lessons you learned from the Marine Corps, you can do it. There's no such thing as failure.

"You look at our history. Am I proud of what I did? No.

"I'm proud that I served my country. Yes.

"I'm proud that I saved lives. Yes.

"I'm not proud that to save life, I took human life. When I think about it, I can even at times have a tinge of sadness and sorrow for the families of those I took. There were survivors, no doubt, of the men I killed. Okay, I know they were our enemies, and their families would have hated us too. But they were soldiers doing their duty, just like me. Soldiers that never came home.

"Every day, I still remember. I will always."

Phil: "Do you think the school and Carlos, that they had you prepared? Unequivocally prepared?"

Mike: "I mean, for the emotional side, he says, 'After your first kill, you're going to throw up your guts. You're going to get drunk, and you're going to think, "What the hell am I doing here?" That's just a natural reaction. More than likely, you're going to have seen a man's head explode in your scope.'

"'Keep this in perspective: you are here because God has blessed you with being here. You're here because the Marine Corps has discovered your gift. And every time you are successful, you are saving lives.'

"I believe all of that is true. Still, it's impossible to erase what I saw happening to those individuals I targeted. Carlos said that would happen."

Phil: "It's interesting that Carlos was talking faith."

Mike: "Hey, Carlos was a Christian. He was a hillbilly redneck. Those people are very religious.

"Carlos's dad taught him hunting/shooting in the hills of Arkansas as a kid, same as my dad. At our school, Carlos made us all feel like family. He was an accomplished shot when he went into the Marines. Just like us, he had to get his head around this whole thing. His upbringing was his backbone. I mean, for him it was God, family, Marine Corps. God, family, Marine Corps was his doctrine.

"He told us how he lived with what he had done. He was familiar with taking a life. Many times familiar. It helped."

Phil: "Let's go back to that first assignment. Tell us what happened."

Mike: "We went out together. I had my sniper rifle. He had his. We each made our shot.

"We went to a blind that he had used before to watch for patrols moving about out near a well-traveled trail.

"Before we go out, in our briefing, he says, 'If we see someone, we're not going to shoot right away. We're going to wait. I don't ever shoot anything under three hundred yards out because I don't want them to be close enough to be able to have any idea of where I am. Usually, I'll wait to shoot the last guy in line as they walk away. Not the first guy, the last guy. That way the other guys will already be some distance away. They'll wonder where the shot came from and probably not even see him tumble when that trailing guy drops. When his buddies turn toward the recoil, they won't know where the heck the shot came from.'

"When we got into position and waited, it turns out we happened to spot a two-man patrol. No one else.

"He signals to me. He points at me, points at the guy in the rear. Points at himself, points at the lead. We synced up and took aim.

"We both sight in. He's a little behind me watching me move. I nod and shoot the one in the rear; he shoots the one in the lead. Like boom, boom. That was it."

"He smiled at me. I smiled back. Hoorah!"

"In seconds, sure enough, just like Carlos had said, I was leaning over in the blind, barfing.

When we get back, he tells the lieutenant, 'He's ready. He's Carlos trained and ready.'"

Note to reader: Did you feel Mike's intensity? Now that you've taken the time to read it all, do yourself the favor of going back to "The Final Conversation" and "Thanks and Appreciation" chapters to revisit those closing conversations once more. He did all he could. Enjoy.

GLOSSARY

ADF (Automatic Direction Finder) – A lower-frequency aviation navigational aid; a directional arrow on the instrument panel shows location angle.

Billet – Where you sleep and keep your gear.

KP – Kitchen Patrol. Just like at home, do the dishes, pots, and pans; get food ready; serve it; stay to clean it all up. Repeat. Usually, KP duty lasts a week.

LAWS (Light Anti-Armor Weapon) – Shoulder-fired antitank rocket. Once fired tubes are often discarded in the field. Our enemies picked them up when they found a grenade fit the tube just right to let them create a hanging tube/grenade booby trap.

MOS (Military Occupational Specialty) – Four-digit number that identifies a service member's primary duty.

NCO (Noncommissioned Officers) – Enlisted troops, corporal and above.

Platoon – Basic infantry unit. Three squads. Each squad a minimum of twelve to fifteen Marines. With command NCOs and officers, fifty total.

Quonset Hut – WWII-era buildings erected for wartime needs, many later converted for other uses. They have an arched half-circle corrugated roof forty or so feet long.

TACAN (Tactical Air Navigation System) – A directional arrow on the instrument panel shows location angle and distance from reference points.

VOR (Very High Frequency Omni-Directional Radio Navigation) – A directional arrow on the instrument panel shows location angle.

Helicopter flight controls:

Collective – The power lever for helicopters. It's mounted to the floor to the left rear of the pilot's seat with a pivot point. When lowered or at rest, the rotor blades have no pitch or lift. As the lever is lifted, pitch increases, adding lift equally to the rotor blades until the lift provided eventually exceeds the weight of the aircraft, lifting it airborne first into a hover, and when ready increasing pitch allows for forward flight. Increasing collective increases lift and "bite," giving the aircraft more speed. Lowering the collective reduces bite, lift, and speed.

Cyclic – The steering lever for helicopters. It's a vertical "stick" mounted to the floor between the pilot's legs on a ball pivot allowing movement in any direction. At its top is a pistol grip with multiple buttons and switches. They control radios, rockets, and aircraft control systems. Moving the cyclic causes the rotors to "bite" more in the direction steered while "biting" less in the opposite.

Rudder pedals – At the pilot's feet on a pivot point allowing the pilot to vary the push-pull of the vertical tail rotor to offset the range of torque forces the spinning main rotors imposes on the airframe.

Acknowledgements

Many people have influenced my life and writing. Most important, Debra. Thank you, baby!

Others: Jeremy, Matt, Erin, Kyle, Greg, Rosann, Barb, John-Paul, Paul, Pauline, Doug, Rita, Bob, Jon, Dave W, Dave H, Chip, Rudi, Sally, Grant, Laurie, Bob and Jan W, Jerry F, Jim W, Tony, John D, Kaitlin, Bart, Nancy, John T, Jeff W.

Marines I knew and tried to stay up with: Capt. Corley, Maj. Bailey, Maj. Clapp, Col. McGinnis. S/Sgt. Stevens, Gunny Barnett. Pilots: Glen Hensley, John Genduso, Wayne Nolan, Charlie Crawford and a bunch more.

Writer role model: Lawrence Colby.

Special thanks to the team at Elite Authors.

Made in the USA
Middletown, DE
29 October 2023

41492669R00120